That Yank With the Crystal

The International Dowsing Journey of an Animal Communicator

BILL NORTHERN

www.honeyhousehive.com

That Yank With the Crystal

The International Dowsing Journey
of an Animal Communicator

BILL NORTHERN

Acknowledgments

My Angels and I would not have developed this gift without God's help and the things I was taught by many dowsers. The purpose of this book is to let everyone know that they too, if they are willing to practice, can become animal communicators.

I would like to thank the lady vet whose husband was a literary agent for giving me the idea to write a book.

Carolee Johnson transcribed many stories from tapes. Pam Bragg typed many stories as I told them. Many others including my daughters Debbie and Cathie also typed stories. Cathie had a friend in Atlanta who put my dowsing class on You Tube. An old friend Arlene Childs also helped us.

Beth at *The Chronicle of the Horse* was also very helpful by publishing articles about how we had helped many horses and by encouraging us to write.

Mr. David Jett at the Richmond County Museum, to whom we will donate all profits from the sale of this book, was also quite helpful.

John Hayes was instrumental in convincing me to shift to Lexington, Kentucky, around 2000. He told me, "You need to be where the horses are."

Princess Abigail Kawananakoa and her ranch manager Wayne Shizuru allowed me to make A-Tri-K Ranch in Waimanalo my headquarters while in Hawaii.

Cindy Comer and Kea Among were valuable in taking bookings and when necessary, driving me around.

Fred and Faye Fletcher were my first contacts in New Zealand as Fred trained for Sir Roy McKenzie, owner of Royden Lodge a leading standardbred breeder in New Zealand.

Michael Ward, a builder, helped me immensely with my rental houses. When a well driller wanted to drill in a different location on Michael's farm than I had marked, because he didn't think water there would be very good, Michael told him, "Bill Northern marked that spot and that is where you will drill!" Turned out to be the best well in West Melton according to the well driller later.

Ann Butts loved to hear what the horses had to say and drove me around Canterbury everyday to listen.

Bill Northern, July 2021
Warsaw, Virginia

Table of Contents

The Starting Gate

Hawaii & New Zealand

Clerk of the Course

Bill Northern's Dowsing School

The
Starting Gate

MY FIRST DAYS OF DOWSING

One day at my store, Wardico, Inc., in Warsaw, Virginia, both bathrooms stopped up. When you have three women working for you, you must have bathrooms! I called all three local plumbers and they could not get to it for at least one week. I knew that there was a cut-off outside of the building, but I wasn't sure where the sewer line was.

So I called the Town of Warsaw and asked them if they could come out and help me locate the sewer line. Since they were just across the street, they came right over with an electronic unit and found something, but it wasn't what we were looking for. So they came back with another tool and they found something, but it still was not what we were looking for.

Next they came over with "L-Rods." These are metal rods that are shaped like an L. It turns out that where the L-Rods crossed was exactly where the sewer line was. I asked them if I could try and they handed me the L-Rods. Sure enough, they worked for me, too! I was so excited. Since the second grade, I had wanted to do something like this. I had tried by using tree branches and it never seemed to work for me. I probably wasn't holding them correctly. The town had a plumbing snake and since the blockage was outside the building, they cleared it for us.

A Journey Begins at the Warsaw Library

That same day, as soon as the town people left, I went to the local library and picked up a couple of books on dowsing. One of the books was *The Divining Hand* by Christopher Bird. The other book noted that there that there was an American Association of Dowsers and they had a convention in Vermont every year. I wrote to the association the next day and asked for more information. I found out that the convention was held every year and now was being held in Lyndonville, Vermont. I found out the details and sent in my deposit right away. It was held in the month of August and I was really looking forward to this trip.

1994 Dowsing Conference in Vermont

We had to fly into Burlington and then drive two and a half hours away to get to Lyndon State College, where the convention was being held. We first went to the hotel and checked in, then we went to the college and picked up our credentials for the next day. When the dowsing classes started. The first two days were a Basic Dowsing Course and on the first day, we spent all morning listening to people talk about dowsing. It was actually kind of boring to me. In the afternoon, they handed out L Rods to all of us and we could go out and find different things on the campus, like water lines, electric lines, etc.

The next day was more serious. We were given a map of the campus and we were expected to mark on a map where the electric and water lines were. Then we brought the maps back to the instructor for a grade. Then, we were given the job of finding any shorts in the wiring of the buildings. We had to walk around three buildings and see if there were any places where the wiring was not installed correctly. Ann and I were able to locate where the wiring was not done correctly right off the bat. Then they gave us the fuel lines that ran underground to find and we were supposed to mark them on a map, too. I don't recall finding them, but we found some of them. We received a diploma that said that we had passed Basic Dowsing School. The certificate was signed by the three teachers.

A Life Changing Moment for Bill

The next day was a true life changing moment for me: A lady brought in two horses. This was the first time that they had ever allowed anyone to bring in horses and they have not done it since. There was a group of students and we were standing approximately 200 feet away from each horse. We had a list of 20 questions, the same question for each horse. The questions were included:

Does this horse like women?

Does this horse like children?

Does this horse have a bowed tendon?

Does this horse have a sickle hock?

Does this horse like to swim?

Like jumping?

Like to pole bend, barrel race, dressage?

We had two sheets, one sheet for each horse. We were all using either our pendulums or our L Rods to answer each question. Since the horses were so far away, you couldn't see them to tell whether or not, for instance, they had a bowed tendon. So you had to rely solely on your pendulum or L-Rods. I didn't do so well; I think that I got five right on one horse and seven right on the other one. This was my very first day of dowsing and as usual, I am a very slow thinker.

That night, I began to think about all of the people that got 17 or 18 right. Most of them were from New York City and probably didn't know a horse from a cow so they *had* to be relying on their dowsing tool. Once this happened, I realized that although I owned horses, I didn't truly *know* them. I was paying around $2000 per month in veterinarian bills and they didn't really know any more about where my horses hurt than the trainer did. This was when it hit me and I realized that this is what I had been looking for all of my life. I could take the guess-work out of diagnosing the problems with horses and all animals and save them from having to put up with an unpleasant trip from the vet and also, in many cases the owners could save thousands of dollars.

STRAIGHT FROM THE HORSE'S MOUTH

The year was 1994-95, and I was at the barn with Bernice Scott, helping her take care of her brother Herbert's horses in Warsaw. I walked past this one horse in particular and heard a voice say, *I didn't get my apple today.*

I looked around to see who had come into the barn. No one was there. I thought I must have been just hearing things. Then, a few seconds later, I heard it again, I *didn't get my apple.* Puzzled, I just stood there and I heard it again, *She forgot to give me an apple.*

I called to Bernice and told her that Freeholder said he had not had his apple that morning. She looked at me like I was crazy and said, "Yes, he did."

Freeholder said in a very sad voice, *No, I didn't either.*

We went on about our day and a little bit later on, it must have hit her. "Bill, you are right, I didn't give Freeholder his apple! How did you know?"

This was the first time but definitely not the last time, that a horse spoke to me. I had been given a gift!

DOWSING IN NEW ZEALAND

For many years dowsing or divining was defined as looking for water and pretty much limited to this. Then it was discovered that dowsing could also be used to find deposits of gold and silver as well as gemstones. My first experience with this was listening to some of the old timers in New Zealand talking about how the divines could go to any map of the area and mark the deposits on the map. They would then go to the site to walk over the selected area to find the best place to mine. Later, they could fly over the mountains with their dowsing rods at the area and mark the area that way. In the more modern area, dowsers are used to help locate oil several miles under the surface. There are seemingly no limits to the information that you can gather by dowsing!

Learning to Dowse Horses

The same year I read in the book, *The Divining Hand* by Christopher Bird, I went to New Zealand and stayed a few weeks near Christchurch. I met Fred Fletcher through Sir

Roy McKenzie, a noted Kiwi standardbred breeder. Fred trains standardbred horses and also does chiropractic work on them in the afternoon. Fred knew that I had only a little knowledge of horses, even though I had owned, raced and bred them.

One summer evening after tea (every meal in New Zealand is referred to as "tea"), I was teaching Fred how to dowse for water. We were able to find the stream that his well was on, as well as the underground electric and water lines. Fred was a bit skeptical but also impressed that he could locate these with his dowsing rods. We were telling him about all of the things that he could use dowsing for. When I mentioned diagnosing horses ailments his eyes lit up! Fred looked at me and said, "You can do that now."

"Do you really think so?"

"Sure," he said.

'The Yank with the Crystal'

The next morning when I went down to the barn, Fred sent someone out to the pasture to bring in two horses for me to go over. While Fred and the trainer went out training two other horses, I went over the other two. We wrote down what we found and when Fred came in he confirmed our findings. We were very fortunate to be staying with Faye and Fred as every afternoon people would bring in a few horses for Fred to treat. This was great experience for me as I would stand outside the stall with the pendulum swinging and asking questions of the horse while Fred was going over them with his hands.

Most of the time, after Fred's examination and treatment, he would ask me what I found. We would then have a short discussion before the next horse arrived. Every evening after tea, we would discuss some of the horses that we had worked with during the afternoon. We agreed on most things, but there were almost always some differences. I learned a lot from these discussions with Fred. In what I do, the way that you ask the question is very important and Fred helped me state the questions in a better way. After about a week, people would ring Faye and ask if the "Yank with the crystal" was going to be there. We were fairly busy that year in New Zealand, but when we returned home in the U.S., no one would believe that we could actually communicate with a horse or any other animal. Some actually looked upon it as "witchcraft." One of my old friends said that when they tied me to the stake that he was going to "light the first match!"

A Buzz Begins in New Zealand

The next year, our visit to New Zealand was much more exciting, as the *Guardian,* a 140-year-old newspaper, published a story about us and we were busy from then until the day we left for home. The trotting and pacing horses in New Zealand have about four weeks of stake races beginning in October and ending with the finals in November. The finals are all raced in what is called "cup week." The races are held in Christchurch and horses come from all over the country to compete in these races.

How a Horse Trainer Became a Believer

One day a trainer that had shipped five horses to the South Island asked me to help him select the best trainer to send each horse to. These horses were all scheduled to race at Christchurch in stake races during cup week.

We dowsed several trainer's names over each horse and came up with the horse's preference. When we were done, I asked the trainer why he chose me to do this for him and why he thought it would work.

He told me a story: He'd used some people on the North Island that did almost the same thing that I did. Using a saliva sample, they would go over, or dowse the horse to find out what was wrong with it. The same as we do. The only difference is they used the radionics machine and I use a pendulum. He was still skeptical back then, so he sent them saliva samples from horses and also himself. In other words, he gave a horse's name to associate with *his own* saliva sample, and sent it in with the rest of the horses' samples.

When the results came back, he went right to the results of the name that he had used for his own saliva sample. The report read, "This horse is terribly overweight." (He weighed about 280 pounds.)

"This horse does not get anywhere near enough exercise." (He did very little work.)

"This horse seems to be close to someone who smokes a lot because his lungs are filling with a brown sticky substance. The person this horse is close to is giving him too much beer or other alcoholic beverages and it is affecting his whole body, particularly his brain."

The trainer finished his story to me with a smile and said, "After that, I will believe almost anything you people tell me." After reading the report, he had gone on a diet, quit smoking and drinking, and eventually lost 100 pounds.

A Growing Reputation

We continued on in New Zealand and were going to horse farms that asked for help with as many as 30 horses. We were only charging $20 a horse at a time. These breeders would usually ask us to select the yearling fillies that we thought would make the best broodmares. We were actually very good at this. Our demand was growing on the South Island but we were not known on the North Island yet.

Business was still very slow in the U.S. There was a standardbred trainer in Warsaw, Virginia, that would let me go over his horses anytime I wanted, but he did not want to pay for my services. I kept thinking that he would see the value of what we were doing, but if he did see the value he never let us know it. The third year, I told him we would have to charge him $10 per horse and then he only wanted for us to work with one or two a week, but he expected us to come every day.

BECOMING ESTABLISHED

The public TV station WCVE in Richmond, asked if they could do a feature with us for a series called, *Virginia Currents.* We thought this would be great. They came down and filmed the feature one hot day in July. It was following spring before they aired it. This segment has aired several times and until recently no one every said they saw it and we have yet to get our first client because someone saw us on that show. Television gets people's attention but unless it is seen many times, people don't seem to want to call the station to get in touch with you.

Becoming established at this is not easy. It seems the real horse people that study every movement of their horses can't believe this is possible. It is always disappointing when you finally gain the trust of a noted trainer then he or she will not tell anyone else about your abilities. The race horse people would say that I am their edge and they did not wish to enlighten their competitors.

Sometimes we will encounter a friendly group of rivals and they will tell each other about us, but not very often. Most of the people that we reach only want to use this for themselves and perhaps their friends. I have taught people that do not help their brothers or sisters if they are competing.

There are still people that believe this strange power is of the devil. These people usually see anything they do not understand as being from the devil. This bothered me at one time, but no longer phases me. I have learned to read and study the Bible for myself. By doing this, I have found several references to the work we do now being done by Jesus and others of His time and before miraculous deeds. Jesus said, "If they are not against you, they are for you."

Every now and then you will come across a person that will tell a lot of people about you. These people are often teased by their peers as going "off their rocker" so to speak.

We have had the most success with the Grand Prix jumping horses and the hunter jumpers as far as people being willing to tell others about us. I think possibly the reason for this is because jumping horse owners look at their horses as being an investment rather than a commodity. They also get along with each other better.

When working with these jumping horses and you find a sore place or something wrong, the owner would ask us what we thought was the best way to treat the problem. If we thought that there was something they could do that would help, they would get working on it massaging, rubbing, etc. Often they would take our suggestion before we could even get to the next part of the horse.

In contrast, if it was a race horse, they would write down what you found and then ring the vet to come and give an injection. Huge difference, and you know why? Show horses, or jumping horses, are usually cared for by their owners and are considered to be part of the family, whereas, race horses are deemed as a commodity.

It would not be unusual to enter a horse barn and have the first horse that you would see not want to communicate with you because he thought that you were a vet. When you find a horse that wants to talk to you and tells you all of his problems, then all of the other horses in the barn stick their heads out and want to see you to talk to you!

I have on several occasions gone to race horse barns and had a vet just follow along behind us, always keeping well behind, treating the horses for the problems we found. Most of these horses hate to see the vet come because they know they are going to get a needle and be hurt in some way. Very few vets that work with horses have a good bedside manner. They are all in a hurry and walk in, do their thing, and walk out as quickly as possible. You would be amazed if you knew about all of the shots, injections, food additives, and other things many race horses have syringed into their mouths or tubed into their stomachs.

Testimonial

Bill Northern & His Angels, Truly Inspirational

My 12-year-old brown thoroughbred mare had suffered a devastating accident four months prior to meeting with Bill Northern, which had left her with a broken right shoulder and various dislocated and misaligned body parts which required many thousands of dollars worth of treatment and care. Eli, as she is called, suffered from periods of depression after the accident followed by bouts of panic attacks and self-mutilation, resulting in serious injuries as she threw herself into fences and gates. I struggled with the option of having Eli put down or not and when I heard of Bill Northern, I decided if he said that Eli wanted to die, then I would have my best friend destroyed.

When I contacted Bill, all that I told him was that I had a horse for him to look at to dowse. When Bill arrived, he just walked up to, but did not touch the horse, just speaking to Eli in a calming tone. Eli didn't trust strangers, but sensed that Bill was going to help and wasn't going to hurt her, so she stood calmly. As I asked questions of Bill's angels, it became apparent that Eli did not want to die even with the 3-4 inch (7.5-10 cm) break of the right shoulder and several sore muscles about her body, all of which Bill pinpointed without me having to tell him.

The main question that I asked of Bill's angels was whether or not Eli would get in foal and his answer was, "Yes, she wants to be a mother." He could see no physical problems within her to prevent this and even said that he could see a foal or foals in the future, of which all would be easily handled and trained. All of this was back in February 1999 and now Eli is in foal to Maestro, a Swedish Warm Blood, which to me is a miracle as she would not get in foal for her previous two or three owners. Bill said that she would only get in foal for me. Bill described the accident which broke Eli's shoulder emphasizing that Eli, in no way, blamed me for what happened and also it wasn't her fault either. I always blamed myself for the accident even though deep down I knew that I couldn't have stopped the two kids from doing what they did to drive Eli into the hard ground.

Shortly after the accident, we still didn't know if Eli had broken her shoulder and she wasn't letting the pain show. Eli appeared stiff but still worked for me so we took her to a ridden show, where she took three 5th place [wins].

Two days after the show, Eli's guard was let down and she let the pain show full force. I had always felt guilty for this but she didn't hold it against me. It was Eli's will to win and her desire to do everything she could for me which kept her going until it, the pain, became too much. By the time Eli had her break diagnosed, she had seen six vets, a chiropractor, an osteopath, and a holistic professional, which helped with some, but not all of her problems, especially the problems with depression or anxiety.

Bill showed me areas to be treated with cold treatments, aloe, arnica. How to massage for her sore bits and pieces. Time was the main ingredient with patience and positivity, all of which would aid Eli's recovery.

Bill gave me an insight into my connection with Eli, which according to Bill, Eli and I are like twins as close as anyone could be. We are one. Even with Eli having a high ability at dressage, we are matched and Eli liked the way that I rode her and I wasn't over horsed like Bill said that a lot of people are. Bill also marveled at the superior level of intelligence which Eli possessed far greater than most people. It is all thanks to Bill Northern and his Angels that Eli is alive, well, in foal and with the future ahead of her and a little bit brighter.

Bill Helps with Nugget

If only more people would open their minds and their hearts to a greater understanding with their horses, they there would not be so many horses around with people problems. Bill's ability also improved the quality of Nugget's life. Nugget is a four-year-old colored ewe, which wasn't her usual self. She seemed grumpy one minute and distant the next so I knew that something was wrong. Nugget is trained like a dog even though she is a sheep. She can jump fences, fetch, shake hands and round up sheep in the paddock, she works on whistle command.

When Bill checked Nugget out he found she had an inflamed and upset liver which he recommended a weeks course of cider vinegar, which cleared up her ailment quickly and Nugget soon returned to normal.

When dowsing Nugget, Bill also picked up on the fact that Nugget enjoyed her runs up the road with me every second or third day and that although, he himself found it, hard to picture Nugget thoroughly enjoyed it and that's what is important.

Bill Northern is inspirational, eye- and mind-opening. It is so uplifting just to talk to someone who can help bridge the gaps between yourself and your animals, a greater understanding can't help but develop with this help.

It is not only horses that would have fewer people problems, but all animals in general be it a cat, dog, sheep, etc. Since I myself, have tried dowsing it opens up many a locked door when faced with injuries that won't heal, problems with new feeds, likes and dislikes of animals who couldn't otherwise let you in on the details of their problem and an answer to help fix it or aid in the solution.

Sarah Caudill

28

Hawaii

&

New Zealand

In Royal Company:
MEETING DAVID KAWANĀNAKOA

I met a girl at a Dowsing Conference that lived in Hawaii. She thought she could get some business for me if she let people know ahead of time that I was coming. She placed signs that read, "Bill Northern Is Coming Here" with her phone number and the dates that I would be there.

When you arrive in Hawaii coming from New Zealand, you always arrive at night. I would call her when I arrived at my hotel. She would schedule my pick-up time and take me to the places that she had horse dowsing sessions lined up for me. One of the first places we went to was A-Tri-K Ranch, which is owned by the Princess Abigail Kawanānakoa. Her nephew, David, and his wife Eleanor were living there. At this point, I did not realize that David was a member of the Hawaiian Royal Family. They had a few horses there for us to look at that day and one of the horses belonged to David's wife, Eleanor. When I first arrived, I asked the horse a series of questions, such as,

"Please tell me if you are sore anywhere."

Eleanor's horse told me where he was sore and he was also telling me that she didn't ride him very often. She said that she rode him every day. Then the horse told me, *No, she doesn't!*

Eleanor said, "Well, almost every day."

The horse said, *No. She doesn't!*"

Eleanor finally admitted to only riding the horse two or more times per week. The crowd, including Eleanor and David were standing around. (I always check with the person that is paying for my services and have them approve who can and cannot be present for my sessions. They must be quiet because I cannot be distracted by noise.) With Eleanor's horse, we found out exactly where he was sore, the nutrients and vitamins that he was lacking, etc.

The next horse that we saw that day was owned by Kea Among, the lady that hauled horses back and forth from the boat yard or the airport. The horse was named Booger, and he *was* a booger. Very naughty. He said he was a prince and wanted to be called that. They immediately began calling him

Prince and the next day he was a different horse.

33

DINNER WITH DAVID KAWAWĀNANAKOA

I decided to stay at The New Otani Hotel in Hawaii when I returned from New Zealand in the late 90's. When I checked in, it was late. The people at the front desk asked me if I would like to have a breakfast reservation. I told them no thank you, I didn't think a reservation was necessary and also I was tired and didn't want to commit to a specific time to eat. The next morning when I went down to get breakfast, the restaurant was completely full. I realized then that I should have made a reservation. The male host of the dining room totally ignored me for a long time, and finally he said that I could have breakfast at the bar if I wanted to. No one else was at the bar, but I was hungry, so I went there and ate alone. That day, I called my friend David Kawanānakoa and invited him to have dinner with me the following evening. I had met him at the A-Tri-K Ranch and had known him for a while. David said that he and his wife could come down the next day for dinner. I went to the front desk to make a reservation (since I learned my lesson with reservations by now!) and told them that David Kawanānakoa was coming to dinner with me. So that evening David and his wife, Maria, were due to arrive for dinner at 7 p.m. I was up in my hotel room and around 6:30 the phone rang and the girl at the desk said, "Mr. Northern, a table has opened up by the ocean, would you be available to come and sit there until Mr. Kawanānakoa arrives? If not, we will have to give it to someone else."

I went down and sat at the table right by the ocean, the best table in the house. I waited there half an hour for David and his wife. The service was impeccable; we were treated like royalty. The Hawaiians obviously adored David. After dinner, David and Maria left and I stuck around for a while. The rest of my stay at the Otani Hotel changed that evening. If I made a reservation, they would say, "Of course, Mr. Northern." I went from being ignored and sitting at the bar by myself to being treated like a king. I ran into a cab driver that evening after dinner and he told me that David would be considered the King of the Hawaiian People today if the monarchy was in effect. I knew that he was a member of the Royal Family but I didn't know just how important he was. David has never acted like he was better than anyone else, just a nice guy who enjoyed life to the fullest.

THE CHIEF JUSTICE
&
HIS DOG ANGEL

My friend David Baba had put me in touch with the judge's wife and I was to listen to their dog named Angel. Angel was a little white dog with big brown eyes, similar to a Bijon. As a judge, he and his wife do a lot of entertaining in their home. Angel would be nice to some guests, but not nice to others. The reason that they wanted me to talk to her was to find out why she was nice to some people, but not other people. Angel told me that the reason that she was not nice to some people was because, *The judge really didn't like them anyway.* She was trying to make them uncomfortable so that they wouldn't come back any more. The interesting thing is that his wife, Stella, was denying that they felt that way about any of their guests. Angel insisted that they did. Later we discovered that the ones that Angel disliked, the judge and his wife were not fond of either. They just invited them over out of obligation. I had only listened to Angel while Stella was present and had not yet been introduced to the judge. But the judge thought that if I could pick up on what Stella was thinking that accurately, then I could possibly help him with a problem that he had. I told him I would. At this time, I was staying in downtown Waikiki and the judge told me to stand on a certain street corner and wait for his call. So I did what he asked and stood on this certain street corner waiting for his call. He called and told me to be on the look-out for a black stretch Lincoln Continental Limousine. Around one minute after he called me, the car pulled up to the curb. The chauffeur got out of the car and asked, "Are you Mr. Northern?"

He then opened the door for me to get into the vehicle. I had no idea why I was being picked up. But I got in anyway. The judge was in the back of the limousine facing me and we proceeded to be driven around. He was asking me general questions regarding his dog Angel, life in general, how was I enjoying Waikiki, etc. No specifics. This continued for a few minutes. At this point, I began to lose my patience and questioned him as to why he was asking me all of these vague questions.

Finally, he said, "Bill, I have a problem in my office. Someone is leaking information and I need your help in finding out who it is." He said the information that was exchanged in and out of his office was supposed to be top secret.

So I closed my eyes and to see if I could come up with anything or anyone that was leaking the information. Shortly after, I saw a woman and I was able to describe how she looked, well enough for him to know exactly who I was talking about. In the government, it's difficult to fire anyone, so he demoted her to the basement. Problem solved! She no longer had access to any private information. He invited me to come to dinner at a restaurant along with some of his friends. Everyone knew him when he walked through the door. But he told no one about me.

BOBBY CHONG'S LOST DOG

Two of my clients had kept horses at Bobby Chong's mother's place in Waimanalo, Hawaii. Since they had me come out to see their animals each year, Mrs. Chong was familiar with what I did, even though I didn't actually work for her. Mrs. Chong's son, Bobby, had a dog missing and she told him that she thought that I may be able to help him. I was already back home in Virginia when this happened.

Bobby and his partner, Curtis, had two dogs. One day, one of them jumped out of the truck while Curtis was driving. Bobby called me to see if I could look for the dog remotely from my home in Virginia. He gave me the location of where the dog jumped out of the truck and I began to dowse and see where he was. I found the dog on the edge of a park, but whenever I looked through the dog's eyes, it was always dark. Bobby figured that the dog must be hiding somewhere in the daytime and coming out into the park at night. So he slept in the park for a few nights, hoping that his dog would show up. He called me every day and had me look for the dog again. Every day I found the dog in the same spot on the edge of the park and from looking through his eyes, I could tell that he was still in the dark. I couldn't figure out why it was dark every time that I looked through the lost dog's eyes. This puzzled Bobby and me. I knew that the dog was being fed and taken care of, but his exact location was still a mystery.

One day, a colleague of Bobby's who was an attorney, had some papers to be signed at a home near the park where Bobby had been sleeping. When his colleague arrived at the house, the owner told him that there was a dog under the porch of his house and that a neighborhood kid had been feeding and bringing him water. Bobby's colleague called him and told him about the dog under the porch. The dog wouldn't come to him so Bobby headed straight over. It turned out that it was Bobby's dog that was hiding under the porch near the park in the dark. Another happy reunion!

BOBBY LEARNS
TO USE L-RODS

Bobby's dog got lost another time. At this time, Bobby was not familiar with L-rods and I had to explain what they were and how to use them. Bobby told me where the dog had left from and sent a map of the area to me. I found his dog on the side of a mountain where wild pigs run. Bobby feared that his dog would be shot by pig hunters. So I told Bobby that his dog was alive and where I thought that he was. Then, I told Bobby to take his dowsing rods and ask to be shown which direction his dog was located. He listened to me.

He used his dowsing rods to find out which direction that the dog was in. Bobby began to walk through the thick brush and used the rods again and again to see which direction his dog was in. The brush was so thick that he had to use a machete to cut his way through. While he was walking, he would call the dog every now and then. He did this for six hours or so and eventually got close enough that his dog was able to hear him. Bobby found his dog and the dog was not

harmed. It was a very happy reunion!

43

THE BLACK LAB
&
MY HOSPITAL EMERGENCY

We were at the A-Tri-K Ranch in Hawaii seeing dogs for people and a lady drove up with a black lab. The second the dog stepped out of the car, he looked me and told me that he didn't want for me to touch him. I tried my best to communicate with this dog, but he just wasn't cooperating. I tried everything that I knew of to get him to communicate with me, but he wouldn't even look at me. The problem was that he was being very unruly, digging up plants in the yard, jumping in the swimming pool with mud on him, etc. I told her that I was sorry but her dog just wouldn't listen to me at all. This bothered me because this just never happened. The lady paid me anyway and left.

For the next few days, I tried and tried to communicate with the black lab and he wouldn't talk to me. It really bothered me. A few days later, as I was heading up the hill back to the house from the barn and didn't think that I was going to make it. I had to get someone to help me. When I got to the house, I told Wayne that I needed to go to see a doctor. He took me to an Urgent Care and the nurse looked at my eyes and said, "You need to get to the hospital right away."

My Hawaiian Angel

So Wayne called Mae and told her that I had to go to Queens Hospital Emergency Room. Mae drove me there to the hospital and it was packed. Mae was very knowledgeable of the procedures at the hospital, but I was uncomfortable. I believe that it was a full moon that night, so all of the weirdos were there. People were crying, talking to themselves, and talking to people that weren't there. I couldn't take it anymore, but Mae insisted that I wait. She took me over to the corner of the emergency room, turned our chairs about so that we couldn't see the crazy people, the only person that I could see was her and I waited. She stayed there with me the whole time. Finally, we got to see a doctor and at this time it was around 9 p.m.

The put me on a stainless steel table and the doctor was examining me. I recall asking her, "Will I be able to get on the plane back to New Zealand tonight?"

She asked what time my flight left and I told her 11 p.m. She said, "You won't be on a flight to New Zealand tonight and you will be lucky if you are still alive tomorrow morning!"

Mae went up to the room with me and stayed with me. It turned out that I had a bleeding ulcer and needed eight pints of blood. I was a very sick man. The second day, they needed to look into my stomach and see where the blood was coming from. The doctor was very nice and asked if they could put a tube down my throat and look into my stomach. They knocked me out and found where I was bleeding and had to cauterize an ulcer. Ever since then, I call Mae my "Hawaiian Angel." I spent a few days in the hospital and around day three Alice came to see me.

Alice Ensures the Best Care

Alice was a nurse and Nursing Instructor at the

University of Hawaii that knew me because I had taught her how to communicate with animals. She was quite good at it, I might add. Alice ended up going to the head nurse at the hospital and she made sure that I received the best care possible. The staff at Queens Hospital was very good, but once Alice came on the scene, things were a little different. It was an advantage to me to be Alice's friend. My roommate in the hospital was a retired dentist. So I got tickled because he was telling the family members who was going to get what when he died. He wanted to give this property to this one and this building to that one . . . This went on. Finally, one day one of his daughters said to him, "Dad, you sold that property a long time ago and you don't own those buildings anymore either!"

When Alice came into my room, everyone shaped up just like the big boss had just entered. As I was beginning to feel better, Alice arranged for me to have physical therapy to help me get my strength back. I wasn't allowed to leave the hospital until I could walk a certain distance and one day the nurse said, "Bill, you did it!"

They discharged me the next day. Mae picked me up from the hospital and took me over to someone that Wayne knew who was somewhat like a doctor and then back to the ranch. I finally took my flight to New Zealand as I had planned. When I returned to Hawaii, one of the first people that brought their dog to me knew the people who owned the black lab and who gave me my ulcer! They told me that he was still digging up plants, getting into the swimming pool while he was muddy and nothing had changed with him.

FRANCIS
&
THE BLIND HORSE

I met a good horseman named Francis Lau in Waimanalo while I was staying at A-Tri-K Ranch. He was the handyman there and took care of almost all of the maintenance. When I first met him, he kept his blind horse at the next ranch down which was called Roberta's. This horse trusted Francis. Francis would tell the horse, "Bushes are here, this is smooth, we are about to go up a hill," etc., in the manner you might talk to a blind person. The horse would understand. Francis could even take the horse on trails. Everyone was amazed that this was possible, because one would think that you wouldn't be able to ride a blind horse. Francis was very meticulous in his work, and he explained everything calmly and with patience.

Many people don't think that you can ride a blind horse, but you can. You have to treat them just like a blind person and explain everything to them ahead of time.

Meeting Princess Abigail

I suffered a cerebral hemorrhage around 1999. I returned around 2000 and stayed at A-Tri-K Stables with the manager, Wayne Shizuru. For perhaps two years Wayne took bookings for me and drove me around. About 2001, Wayne introduced me to the Princess Abigail, and I was invited for dinner with her at David and Eleanor's. At this time Abigail was in bankruptcy and Wayne's only income was from giving riding lessons.

I had a private conversation with Eleanor. She was not impressed with me because I knew almost nothing about horses. At this time she was bankrupt and I had little respect for her also. I felt sorry for Wayne having to work for almost nothing. He did not have to pay rent or any household expenses and a truck was furnished for him to drive but it was still a struggle. After about three years Wayne gave up taking my bookings and turned it over Kea Among. Kea did a nice job, but like Wayne, did not accept bookings for me from people she disliked or did not trust. This was probably a good thing, but I did not realize it at the time. I still stayed at Wayne's and went over his horses free in exchange for rent.

Advancing My Studies

Then I went out to New Mexico to take a class on Neuro-Linguistic Programming (NLP). This was very interesting and now I realize that most professional and college teams are using it to convince their players that they are the best and convince the opposition that they are not good enough to be in this league. Around 2004, Miss Abigail came out of bankruptcy and soon after, she received her share of the Campbell estate. This was around 240 million dollars. Along about this time Kekau was going to purchase new Saturn automobiles for all of her employees. Wayne did not want a Saturn. He thought he deserved a Lexus because he had worked for almost nothing for a few years. I began practicing NLP with her to convince her to give Wayne a Lexus. At first her subconscious mind was opposed but after about three weeks I was able to convince her that he deserved the Lexus automobile. She rang him one morning and told him to go and pick it up. This was the beginning of something I had never really considered seriously before. Wayne, since I knew him, had always been very subservient to Kekau and would get very upset if she was mad with him. He was always doing everything he could to stay on her good side, much like a dog will do to keep his master happy. We together decided to use NLP on Kekau to be nicer to Wayne and give him gifts in the way that she was bestowing on some others in her employ and friend circle. The way I was to be compensated was I would get a house on Koa Ridge and 20 percent of anything Wayne received over 100 thousand dollars. Over the years the going was difficult but she gradually accepted me telling her how loyal Wayne was to her and how he deserved extra compensation for being there for her whenever needed. Now Wayne is wealthy because of her gifts and doesn't answer my calls any longer.

TEACHING AT THE UNIVERSITY OF HAWAII – ALMOST

Alice in Hawaii had a friend named Roseanne who was sick in the hospital. Alice brought me a list of all of the medications that Roseanne was taking, it was a lot of medication, probably around 16-17 different kinds. I had taught Alice how to dowse, so she asked if I would dowse the list of medications and see if any of them could be eliminated.

So I did and I came up with reducing her medications to only six. Alice agreed with me and consulted with one of the doctors at the hospital and shared my findings with him. The doctor agreed to remove the unnecessary medications and within ten days, Roseanne was much better and was able to come home! Once Roseanne returned home from the hospital, Alice shared with her that I had dowsed the list of medications that she was taking and had suggested that several of them be eliminated. Around this time, Roseanne asked me to take a look at her dog. He wasn't acting like he used to and she told me that she was paying a man to walk her dog for an hour each day. When I dowsed it, I found that the man was only walking the dog for 15-20 minutes each day. Roseanne consulted with the dog-walker and found out that that was true. We found that the dog needed medication and, of course, she arranged that right away. Since Roseanne confronted the dog-walker, he agreed to walk the dog for an hour from then on.

After this, Roseanne, who was the Co-Dean of the University of Hawaii Medical School, was so impressed with my dowsing of her medications and her dog, that she asked me if we could teach this for a quarter at the University. Alice said, "Sure he can, he taught me!" We began to plan for myself and approximately nine others that had agreed to come and teach at the University for a week in exchange for room and board. We were still in the planning stage when a friend of mine, whose wife was a court reporter, called and said that he thought that we may as well call off the idea of teaching at the University of Hawaii. He said, "Somebody is suing the school and their lawyer in his arguments stated that the school must be desperate for instructors since they were considering having a group of whackos come to teach there like Bill Northern, who calls himself an animal communicator!" Needless to say, that was the end of our teaching experience at the University of Hawaii and the subject never came up again.

Testimonial

June 30, 1999

Meeting Bill Northern was quite an experience for my husband and I. We were not only skeptical, but a little unsure of what he would say or if he would be able to help us. We train and racehorses and we needed a lot of help with some of our horses. It is quite entertaining to hear what your own horses have to say about you, your training methods, the way they are treated, whether they are happy or not and many other things. You may not want to hear everything that he has to say because all horse trainers realize that all of the horses that they have are not going to make good racehorses. You don't always want to hear that, however, it is a fact of life.

Our first meeting with Bill Northern was an experience to remember. There were 10 horses that he was going to talk with that day. We were quite stunned when the second horse that he talked to told him that she did not like her hay. She is a picky eater and is very hard to please. She also constantly kicked the wall and over a period of weeks he talked to her about this. She finally almost stopped doing this and when she did kick the wall, I would tell her that Bill did not want her to do this and she would stop again for a week or two. The fourth horse that he talked to told him that she did not get enough attention. I said, "She gets carrots every day!" The horse said, "I get plenty of treats but not enough attention." Bill also told us that she had bladder problems, which was true.

The first, third and fifth horses that he talked to, basically did not have any problems but he advised us to cull these three because they had low heart scores. This means that they have very little desire to race. By this time, we were amazed because we have discovered this about these three horses and have been trying to decide whether to continue with them or not.

The sixth horse that he talked to was a nervous problem horse. I had been wondering if plugging her ears *would help her. Bill asked her and she told him, "tell her to plug her ears, it won't help me." We all got a good laugh out of that.*

The other four horses that were talked to that day had high heart scores and only minor problems. As Bill told us after talking with them, they have made pretty good racehorses.

One of them told Bill to tell my husband that he was not pleased with the way that he was driven in the race the previous week. We laughed and asked him how he wanted to be driven. He told Bill and that week he won. Bill also asked him if he was spoiled by one more than the other. Everyone knows that my husband spoils the horse terribly.

In the year that we have known Bill Northern he has talked to our horses many times and has given us a lot of good advice. He can talk with them in person or from a distance. We continue to be pleased with our dealings with him and will seek his help in the future.

Sincerely, D.S and L.S.

TONY'S LOST DOG,
MOUSE

I had been working with Cindy Hampton's thoroughbreds for awhile. Her father, Tony Prentiss, had taken his little dog Mouse with him to visit his other daughter in Kaikōura, which is north of Christchurch. He was headed to Wanaka to an airshow and he didn't want to leave Mouse by herself. He didn't tell Mouse where he was going or how long he would be gone. So Mouse broke through the screen door and took off. Cindy told Tony that I may be able to find Mouse for him. I was at home in the U.S. at that time and Tony called me to tell me what had happened.

At that time, I didn't have the ability to print out a map of New Zealand, so he had someone pull up a map of the area and send it to me by email. From the map they sent to me, I was able to locate Mouse who was running through the brush. Tony called me at least twice per day to find out where Mouse was. I kept following her. She had hurt one of her eyes and a day or so later, one of her paws was injured. She was headed to Christchurch and had gone at least 15 miles through rough countryside. Tony posted an award for her in all of the local papers for 1,000. Back then, that was a lot of money to find a dog. Each day, I kept on following her along and I found her at the Clarence River, which is between Christchurch and where she had left from. There was a white house there and she had tried to cross the river, but the current was too strong. I told Tony where she was located and he drove there right away. The people had recognized Mouse and kept her there for him. Both Mouse and Tony were very happy.

Approximately six months later, I visited Tony in New Zealand. I persuaded Tim Nichols, my landlord, to drive me over to see Tony and to meet Mouse. We found the parking lot and before I even got out of the car, I heard something scratching on my door. Mouse was there. She darted away from Tony, which she had never done, and ran out to greet me. She was so excited that she jumped up on me. Keep in mind, I had never met Mouse in person before this. She knew me.

THE KIWI FARMER
WHO BECAME A BELIEVER

There was a man in New Zealand that owned a kiwi farm that rented a shed out to my friend Alister Cox and his partner. Alister and his partner were alchemists and had lots of chemicals in their shed. In this shed, they had lots of different size tanks and would mix the chemicals in different tanks, depending on how much they needed for a particular job. The kiwi farmer would load up the tanks on his forklift and put them into his truck and then drive them to the farm the where the chemicals were needed. Kiwi fruit is grown on a trellis. You can walk under it and there are kiwis all around you, over your head and all.

But around two acres of the kiwis were not doing very well at all. The leaves and vines were not as green as they should be and the fruit was very small. He contacted the local extension office and asked for help. They came up with a soil analysis and he asked me if I could tell what the trouble was with the kiwi fruit because the soil analysis didn't pick up on

anything. He was holding a list of all of the components of the

soil and what percentages of different compounds were

present. As he would read off, for instance, phosphorus, I

would dowse and see if the soil had too much phosphorus or

not enough. He would compare what I found to the list he was

holding. We continued down the list and he never said

anything. When we finished, there were only three items that

my dowsing disagreed with the soil test. Two of them were

slight differences, so little that we didn't think it made any

difference. I believe that it was phosphorus that I had picked

up on that the soil didn't have enough of and the sample report

stated that it had way too much phosphorus. We got Alister

and other dowsers to dowse the kiwi fruit and they also came

up with the kiwi fruit not having enough phosphorus. It

turned out that Alister and his partner figured out what to

spray on the kiwi so that the phosphorus that was there was

absorbed by the fruit. It took them a day or so to mix up what

was needed. The next day, they spread the mixture on the soil and within two weeks the plants were green and from then on the kiwi plants produced beautiful full kiwi fruit. The owner of the kiwi farm then became a believer.

THE SOCIETY OF DOWSING & RADIONICS

The New Zealand Society of Dowsing and Radionics is headquartered in Auckland. One day, Alister decided to take me to see the president of the society, Albino Gola. We sat around talking about dowsing for a couple of hours and all that you could do with it. We also discussed the radionics machines and how the U.S. government won't allow them because they "don't work." We talked a lot about energy fields. Alister, of course, was aware of them and able to clear them, as well as Albino Gola. Alister was known by the believers as a very good dowser. On this particular day, we began talking about crystals that he would wrap copper wire around. He had them all over his house to remove negative energy. I can recall him going over to the television to pick up one of the crystals and when he picked it up, his entire arm lit up! Just like a light bulb had been turned on. When the crystals get full of energy, they need to be taken back to the earth or cleansed. Placing them on the ground is usually sufficient. After I witnessed his arm lighting up, we went around the house, we noticed that instead of picking up the crystals with his hands, he used wooden tongs. We helped him place all of the crystals in a box and we took them outside to earth them. When we walked back into the house with the clean crystals, we could all feel a huge difference in the energy of the house. It felt so much better and much lighter. Albino was very gracious for us pointing out that his crystals in his home needed to be recharged by earthing.

JOHNNY LEARNS HOW TO FIND NEGATIVE ENERGY

My friend Alister has a brother named John who was a horse trainer in New Zealand. John was having problems with negative energy around his entire farm. The horses were sickly, lethargic and not doing as well as they should have been. Alister realized that his brother needed some help and the best way to try to clear this negative energy was for he and I to go down there to help him. Alister and I left from Christchurch and drove all the way down to Invercargill to see if we could help John. When we arrived at John's farm, it was late at night and we were tired, so we decided to begin the next morning. John had work to do, so he left us alone. Alister and I began to dowse the negative energy and were able to clear it up, all but one spot. We intentionally left the equipment shed uncleared of the negative energy because John was a bit skeptical of what we were doing. We had tried to show John how to dowse and find the negative energy to clear it. When John's little boy, Johnny, got off of the school bus that afternoon, Alister and I handed him the dowsing rods. John was home by this time and we began to show his son how to do basic dowsing. We had Johnny go to a few specific places to see how the energy was and he didn't pick up on any negative energy, whatsoever. John was observing. Then we took Johnny over to the equipment shed. He immediately located the bad energy. He also spoke of how uncomfortable the negative energy made him feel. As soon as we cleared the negative energy from John's farm that day, everything changed for the better. His horses started racing well and felt better. The entire family felt better. Needless to say, he didn't doubt our dowsing capabilities ever again!

Years later, John's son Johnny had become a harness horse driver. I was at Ken Barron's and he was interviewing a person to help him around the farm and drive his horses. It turned out that the person that he was interviewing was John's son, Johnny Cox. Johnny had remembered us and what we showed him. Ken was also a believer and guess what? He hired Johnny on the spot!

LORD FREDERICK, THE HORSE TRAINER

Sir Roy sent me to see Fred on my second day. **Fred** was a well-known and respected trainer who trained horses on the South Island for Sir Roy, among others. Naturally, Fred and I talked horses. I knew little about horses and inquired as to what one needed in order to purchase a horse in New Zealand. What we call a stall, Kiwis call a box. Fred told me the first thing on the list was to learn to clean the boxes to suit the trainer. He handed me a pitchfork

After doing what I thought was a good job, I called Fred over to check my work. He kicked the shavings around a bit and said, "Here is a piece that you missed,"then another and another. Fred finally said he didn't think the I was qualified to own a horse in New Zealand! Sir Roy suggested that first, I should purchase some property in New Zealand, and then get a horse. With his help, I was able to get a bank loan to buy a house.

THE LOAN OFFICER
WHO DISAPPEARED

Sir Roy McKenzie had suggested strongly to me that I should invest in property in New Zealand because the government was going from a socialistic one to capitalistic. He said that he would help me get financing when I found the house or houses that I wanted to buy. First, I went to the Bank of New Zealand per his suggestion to coordinate financing the purchase of a home. At this time, the New Zealand dollar was only worth 50-cents in U.S. dollars, so the houses were really cheap to me. The loan officer that I was talking to was a young lady, and lunchtime approached. I asked her if she would go to lunch with me and she accepted. We went to a little restaurant called Cobb & Co and we were seated by the window. We ordered our food and were having nice conversation when two flies appeared on the window beside us. They were flying all around our table. As a dowser, I had learned to put a light around us to make it uncomfortable for the flies. When I put up my hand to create the energy field, she said, "What are you doing, Bill?"

I said, "I am creating an energy field for these flies to make them uncomfortable and leave us alone."

She responded, "Could you please excuse me?" I assumed she needed to use the restroom. She never came back.

WARNING MY BROKER
ABOUT A BAD INVESTMENT

I purchased a house through a real estate company and over time, I grew to like the broker very much. He was thinking about purchasing another real estate company in Christchurch and told me a little bit about it. He didn't ask me to dowse it, but for some reason I came up with the fact that it wasn't a good deal. He told me that this company had eight salesman and sold 5-6 million in property last year. When I looked at the company that he wanted to buy, I could sense that only two of the salesmen actually sold anything. He had been given a lot of figures that didn't seem right to me. I told him that he was being given wrong information and that he needed to ask them to see their tax records. As it turns out, the people were keeping two sets of books! They were not as successful as they had told him and he didn't buy the company. He ended up going to another part of New Zealand and bought another company. His business is doing very well.

PENDULUM DOWSING
FOR HARRIS THE RACEHORSE

I saw Harry Weber was sitting at a table at Addington Raceway in Christchurch one evening of racing. Harry looked down in the dumps and I asked what was troubling him. He knew I was a dowser but he wasn't convinced it worked and he still isn't. He told me he had a two-year-old that he was very high on. The vet had come out that day to check his heart score and it was only 110. This is low. I took out my pendulum and dowsed the horse named Harris. I picked up his heart score was 120. Harry looked at me with a grin and said, "Billy Boy, if this horse has a heart score of 120, you will never pay for another haircut in New Zealand."

This was around 1995. Little did Harry realize that I was going to return to New Zealand for 20 more years. At the time, all I knew about Harry was that he was a barber. I did not know that he owned a full block of shops in Merivale, Christchurch, an exclusive area. The next day he had a different vet come to do the heart score. He got 119. Harry

rang the first vet and asked him to do it over. This time he got

120. Harry was a very unusual person. He had been a gunner

on B -29 bomber in the Second World War. He was well-read

and up-to-date on the latest news and events. Very wise man.

He loved classical music, and if he was not busy and you

walked in his shop, he would make you wait until the piece now

playing was over. He would then proceed to tell you how the

composer was feeling when he wrote the piece. Every year

thereafter, I would make it a point to visit Harry's shop for a

free haircut. He was about the most expensive barber in town

but never would take anything from me for a haircut. When I

offered to pay, he always said, "A deal is a deal." He retired in

2014 and is still helping Mark Smolinski train horses and also

training a couple of his.

PLACING LIGHT OVER LYN & MARK MALCOLM'S FIELD

One of the things that we learn through dowsing is how to place an energy field over something to protect it. One day, I was at Mark and Lyn Malcolm's in New Zealand with a small group of my students and we were having a little party. We were talking about all of the things that we could do with dowsing. Mark had two 10-acre fields planted with linseed separated by a shelter belt near Rakaia, New Zealand. We thought it would be very interesting if we put a light around one of the fields to protect the plants from insects and birds. I wasn't able to do this all by myself, so six of us spread out around the field and we all participated in creating a light to protect the plants from insects and birds. We asked Mark to please keep track of what he harvested in each field and to let us know how much our light helped. It turned out that he got about a 12 percent better yield from the field that we had put the light around than from the other field that didn't.

LYN MALCOLM'S
Testimonial

Bill came to my property to talk with my horses. In total I have 17 purebred Quarter Horses. We were in my broodmare paddock this day and I was convinced all my mares were in foal. Bill informed me that one black mare was not in foal, and at that point, I was still hoping he was wrong. But sure enough, she came back into season one week later.

Adjusting My Expectations of a Filly

One particular filly I own, whom I have always respected but never connected with, was immediately identified by Bill. He knew by talking to her that the horse felt I expected too much from her and thought I was a 'cow.' I looked at Bill and then at the horse, laughed and realized that she was right and I had expected too much of such a young horse. From this experience, my attitude toward this filly has changed for the better and we have a better understanding of each other.

These are just two examples of many. Thank you, Bill.

Lyn Malcolm (New Zealand)

DOWSING FOR A FEED STORE IN ASHBURTON

In Ashburton, New Zealand, there was a feed store that served almost everybody in the area. One time, there were two different people that were having trouble with their horses eating the feed that they had purchased there. I found out from talking to the horses and dowsing the feed that it the feed was on the verge of being rancid.

So I went to the store and told the owner that I suspected that he was selling feed that wasn't good. Feed doesn't have a long shelf life, particularly in the summertime. He became concerned and opened a bag of food that was fresh and compared the smell to a bag that we suspected was bad and he could actually smell the difference between the good and the bad feed. So the owner of the store called the manufacturer of the feed and had them pick it up and replace it with fresh feed.

He hired me to go over the rest of the feed in the store to see if there was anymore that wasn't good.

From then on, every year when I went to New Zealand, he had me come dowse all of the feed for freshness. If we discovered that it wasn't fresh, he would call the manufacturer and have them come to replace it. Word got around that this was the best store to purchase food because the owner was doing everything that he could to be sure that the feed was fresh. After the store owner hired me, his sales increased by over 20 percent.

EATING GOOD IN ASHBURTON

A very nice article about our work was published in the Ashburton *Guardian,* which is a daily newspaper more than 140 years old. After that, we received several inquiries. One of these phone inquiries was from a lady with two horses, each ridden by one of her two daughters. We had a chat with her older daughter who was 14 years old. They asked me if I would come and work with their horses. They lived about 40 kilometers from Rakaia. I explained that if I drove that far for only two horses, I would need to charge a bit extra for time and mileage. One day while driving, I received a call from her. She told me that she and her sister were bringing their horses to the Pony Club in Ashburton and was wondering if we could work them in our schedule. I arranged to meet her at the Pony Club around 4 o'clock. As it worked out, the Pony Club was next door to where I would be for our 3 o'clock appointment.

Animal Communication Is for Everyone

We arrived at the Pony Club field and Fay was waiting. The first horse we worked was Fay's sister's. As is customary we had the young lady place her hand on the horse where it told us it was hurting. After a few minutes, she realized that she could put her hands on her horse and feel exactly where the horse was hurting. She was a very sensitive young lady. There was an important horse show that weekend and Fay wanted to know whether to ride her horse or her sister's horse in the competition. We started to go over Fay's horse and then decided to first let her sister go over the horse with her hands. Her sister was very perceptive and with her hands, could feel most of the places the horse was sore. We found out this horse thought that if they would do some rubbing on her and give her the proper exercise that she would be ready for the weekend show. When we finished with the horse I worked with Fay's sister a few minutes to try to help her touch technique. I also tried to teach her a bit about healing with your hands.

The youngster caught on to this quickly but her mother was not sure she wanted her daughter to learn to do these strange things. Her mother seemed to think this was a lot of rubbish. A lady whose daughter was taking riding lessons had been watching and asked if we would have time to work with her daughter's horse. I told her we would be most pleased to try to help her. She then inquired about our charges and when given the figure told me she would need to first go into town to an ATM machine to get some money as she did not have her checkbook with her. I said, "We can work with the horse now and you can pay me later. I am going to eat tonight whether you pay me or not."

The lady who we had just been working for spoke up and said, "You don't have to worry about him, I just paid him enough so that he can eat for a week."

Come to think of it, the other lady never did send me a check.

HOUSE-SITTING
IN NEW ZEALAND

Maury and his wife Ruth were friends of mine that managed Roydon Lodge for Sir Roy McKenzie. Ruth had some friends that were going away for around three months and they needed someone to house-sit for them. They wanted me to pay them 50 per week to stay at their home. I could use their truck, but I had to pay 50 cents per kilometer. When we were first discussing the arrangements, they told me that the only thing that I had to do for them was to water the houseplants. That didn't seem like a big deal. It was a five-bedroom home and the price was very reasonable.

I arrived in New Zealand to meet with them on the night before they were leaving. At this meeting, they had a few more house plants than they had previously told me about. There were plants inside of the house. There were plants on the outside of the house in pots. Also, they had approximately 250 blue gum trees that they had just planted the previous summer that needed water. They assured me that they had a watering system for the trees, but it was not working correctly. The watering system didn't work anything like they said that it would. I had to water everything, including the 250 blue gum trees manually! The watering of all of the trees kept me pretty busy for those three weeks. There was one particular little tree at the back door in a large pot. For some reason – maybe I watered it too much -- it lost all of its needles and was dying. I decided to put a French coil around the tree to help it, and by the time they returned, the tree was healthy and had lots of fresh buds on it.

Spirits in the House

The back door of their house was only about 50 feet from a railroad track. naturally I heard every single train that went by. Day and night. I would wake up in the middle of the night and would hear beautiful music playing on piano. I thought to myself, *I must have left the radio on in the kitchen.*

I would walk by the living room to go to the kitchen to

turn off the radio and the music would stop. This went on every single night and it usually would occur just before a train was coming through. Sometimes during the three months there, I would have some of my dowsing students over. One of my first students was a Maori lady named Jean Calvert. She had her L-rods in her hands and walked down the hallway of the house. Her rods started turning around like a propeller on a helicopter! She said, "Bill, you need to get the hell out of here right now!"

Clearing the Spirits

I had already been aware of the spirits in the house and I had asked them if they were in approval of me staying there. They said there was no problem with me being there, in fact, they liked me. But naturally they were not very fond of some of my students. I contacted Dick Paskowski, a friend of mine that did exorcisms, and asked him if he could come and help me to remove these spirits. Dick lived in Connecticut but agreed to help me remotely. It didn't seem that Dick was very successful, so I contacted my friend Don Huschke and asked him to please give me a hand.

Sometimes it takes two people to clear spirits.

Dick was successful at removing the spirits. It appeared as though they had left the home. I noticed that the music didn't happen anymore at night. My students were now comfortable in the house and I was able to teach them better because they were more relaxed.

A New Ride

One day, John Butts, a mechanic who worked for Fred Fletcher, came by and said that Fred had told him that I may be able to help him with his dog, Cracker.

Cracker was a really good greyhound who had won approximately 50,000, but had recently gone off form. John took me to see him to see if I could find out what was wrong. I mentioned that I was paying 50-cents per kilometer to use their ute. So after I didn't charge John for looking at Cracker, that afternoon he brought a little car over. He told me that we could go for a little ride. The car was a stick shift and so he had to show me how to use it. He said, "Bill, I only paid 600 for this car today and you can have it for that if you want it."

So I bought it. The car had the warrant of fitness for one year. At that time, New Zealand drivers were very courteous. If you were behind someone and needed to pass them, they would just kindly pull over so that you could pass them. Although this car was 20-plus years old, it was in very good condition.

Shortly after this, my friend John passed away from an aneurysm. Every year, I would stop by to see his wife, Ann, to see how she was doing. She was very interested in talking to animals and in how I did it. One year, she told me that I may as well stay with her so that I could teach her how to communicate with animals. She loved to hear what the animals had to say. She drove me all around so that we could listen to the animals. While I was there, her neighbors Dennis and Denise Nyhan would invite me over for dinner once or twice per week and I would listen to their horses. Dennis was from a long line of horse trainers. His two daughters were horse trainers and he was very knowledgeable about the politics of

the horse business.

CLEANING UP WATER

One day at Alister's house we decided to do some water cleaning. So he invited four people over and one of them brought around two liters of polluted water out of a stream that had already been condemned by the state. Our goal was to clean up the water, so, we poured everyone a glass of the polluted water. Then we dowsed the water together, to see what we needed to do to clean it up. Each person dowsed their own glass of water for at least an hour. When you looked at the water, it initially looked clear and clean.

But once we started dowsing, tiny pieces of sediment slowly started to form in the bottom of each glass. This was something that I had never done before. Alister and his friends had done it a few times before, but had never sent it afterwards to be tested. We poured the water into a large container and sent it to be tested by a lab. The results showed that the water was indeed now potable water. I had been a bit skeptical about whether or not the water was really cleaned up, but after the lab results, there was no doubt. At this

moment, I was convinced that anyone who desires to do this

could do it, as long as you were *really* a believer.

THE POSSESSED CAT

Grame Lamb was a standardbred trainer who asked me to teach him and his daughter to dowse. When we were doing the energy we realized that there was a lot of negative energy around his farm. Once they really got into dowsing, it was obvious that this energy was everywhere. We cleared all of the negative energy that we could find.

The surprising thing was that he had a cat that was possessed. Wherever this cat went, everything got out of its way. When the cat walked into the pasture, the horses ran. When the cat went near the dogs, they took off running. I had heard stories about this cat, but after seeing this, I realized that there was a real problem. I called my buddies, Don Huschke and Dick Paskowski and asked them to help me with this one, clearing the negative energy from the land and in particular, to help me with this cat. After they cleared the cat of his negative energy, it disappeared! Never to be seen again. We determined that the cat was the reason that Grame had unfortunate circumstances happen to him. After the cat left, everything got better.

93

Testimonial

Meeting Bill was definitely an experience that I won't forget. My friend Clare and I had heard of this "horse whisperer" guy through the local gossip in our town. I always liked an adventure and to try new things, so we contacted Bill.

Bill arrived on a very warm evening in his little well-traveled car. We didn't know what we had let ourselves in for, as this guy was a large person that came to greet us! All of our worries disappeared as Bill greeted us with a warm smile, the atmosphere became extremely calm, and the horses were very at ease.

My skepticism crept up – even though I had buried it deep inside of me! – and I couldn't help thinking, Was I mad? Was I throwing money away? He's a horse whisperer for God's sake!

But all of my fears were swept aside once Bill started to "talk" to my horse, Henry. Now, I'm one of those people who imagines what their horse would like if he was a human and I had Henry down as a sort of "George Clooney"-- charming, homely, not bad looking, could be a little lazy, could be a baddy with a soft center! Bill "spoke" to Henry by going into a sort of trance (at this point I thought that he must be on a different planet!) and came back with almost the same character assessment. Well, so far, so good, I thought. Now I was going to hit Bill with a good one: "Why doesn't Henry like going into a horse trailer?"

Bill spent a few moments with Henry, then he told me that Henry thought that the trailer was too small. "Well, tough!" I said. "It is the only one we've got!" Now this wasn't a problem that was going to be solved straight away. Bill said he had to spend a few nights talking with Henry from where he was staying and that he would contact me.

Before Bill left, he told me a few things about Henry, which no one except me would know. By now, I was excited and couldn't wait until Saturday when the trailer problem would be solved! It took only half an hour on that warm summer night to convince me that it was money well spent!

Saturday came, I rang Bill to find out the "verdict." Would Henry go into the trailer? Bill burst out laughing an said, "Yes, but I had to talk to Henry, tell him that the trailer was safe and there was enough room."

The big moment came. I had my friend Clare with me (as a witness!). We stood there with the ramp down, not knowing really what to say to Henry. All I kept thinking was, "Please don't let the neighbors hear us, they will think that we have gone soft! I spoke with him softly, explained the situation and told Henry the situation was completely safe. Well, you could have knocked me down with a feather. Henry walked straight on while Clare and I just stood there with our chins on the floor! Henry just turned his head and as if to say, "Well, come on then. What's all of the fuss about?" Needless to say, I was crying it was so fantastic to see a nice calm horse, happy to go on the trailer with not a fight in sight! I will never forget that moment!

Bill has taught me to "speak" to my horse and the results have been rewarding, Bill has a fantastic gift to help others and I cannot wait to meet him again when he comes back to New Zealand.

Sharon Martin and Henry

THE HAUNTED HOTEL

Two of my students, Geoff Dunn and Natalie Mallett took me to the Cafe Izone for dinner. It is the best restaurant in the area and the conversation was interesting. Geoff is a very good horse trainer, as well as an animal listener, and Nat is a good psychic, interested in the horse's well-being. It was an evening well spent. A couple of days later I received a message from my friend Tim Nichols whom I have known for years. Tim has written a new book under the pen name, Kris Jiddhu. In the book he briefly told of us dowsing the property where when we was thinking of leasing it to have a hotel.

At that time, we had found a good deal of negative energy and advised him to not lease that location. But he leased it anyway and a couple of years later, I was in his office and noticed a letter from the Bank of New Zealand which I believed threatened foreclosure on the business. After chatting a while, he admitted things were not going well. Guests who had made bookings months and weeks in advance were walking up to the front desk and deciding they did not want to stay there. The place was nicely decorated and looked to be quite comfortable, but the energy from a person who had lived in part of the building did not want any company. The spirit was that of a man named Britton, I believe, who invented and made very fast motorcycles. I went with Tim to his house and immediately went to the study to try and convert the negative and noxious energy in the hotel to beneficial energy for everyone entering and working at the hotel. I contacted my friends who did exorcisms, Dick Paskowski and Don Huschke to send Mr. Britton to the light for us. We were very successful in this endeavor. For months thereafter the hotel was filling up almost every night. The hotel was successful until the bad earthquakes in 2010. Part of the building was destroyed and severe damage was done to nearby buildings including the famous Christchurch Cathedral.

THE SKEPTICAL TRAINER WINS BIG WITH LITTLE MISS SUNSHINE

A man rang and said we had been highly recommended to have a look at his horse, Little Miss Sunshine, and figure out what her problem was. He collected me about 6:30 p.m. and took me about three miles to where his horse was located. The horse was with a new trainer who had been working with one of the leading trainers in New Zealand before going out on his own. He was very skeptical, as was his wife. But they agreed to listen to what the horse had to say and write it all down. This fellow was a very good trainer but was unable to sort out this horse.

The first thing I asked Little Miss Sunshine was if she wanted to be a racehorse and she said, *No.*

I told the man he did not owe me anything if he wanted to take me home. He asked if I would be willing to give her a good going over to see if she was sore anywhere and if there was anything they could do to get her to change her mind. I agreed and began my usual exam. She was sore in a few places and, I believe had a kidney or bladder problem. Her hooves were all out of balance the way they were trimmed and shod. I stood on each one, using the method taught me by Doug Gray a few years earlier. I told them exactly how she was putting weight on each hoof. They wrote it all down. Then I asked if she would want to be a racehorse if they would fix all of her issues. She said she would like that.

Three weeks later, the phone rang and the caller asked if I had just seen the first race of the day on TV? He said, "Well, the mare Little Miss Sunshine that you worked with a few days ago was in that race and she just bolted in paying 41 to one to win and 19 to 1 for place."

The owner was so pleased with her progress after the trainer had her hooves balanced and her sore places fixed that he bet 500 on her to win and 300 to place. Next the owner rang to thank me.

The satisfaction from doing things like this is fantastic.

TRAINING HORSES
ON THE BEACH

I was off to to see Lou Driver and Robin. This was my first time going the beach to watch the horses work. There is a very long stretch along the ocean in Belcarin, north of Christchurch where where people can come and work their horses and the horses love it. There is something different for them to see every day as the beach changes with the tides. The horses really look forward to going. Lew, Robin, and John put the harness on the horses before leaving home. They just lead them to the large float, or trailer. The horses go on by themselves. We parked about a quarter mile from the ocean, unloaded the horses, hooked them to the cart, the driver hopped in the seat, and off they went across the sand to the ocean. The soft sand helps build some muscles that do not get used much in racing. When they get near the ocean, the sand is packed tighter from the water and they now use some different muscles. There were other trainers at this same location but there is enough beach that there is room for everyone. Robin said she has seen someone in the ocean only once as it is rough, cold, and windy. We went back to the farm and unloaded the horses, then took off all of the harness and walked them a bit to cool out.

I drove Lew into Christchurch to collect an MG he has shipped down from Auckland. He likes the old cars. After dropping him off at the shipping yard, I rode over to see Nat Mallett. We then went to the races at Addington. John McDermott's horse Fly Over was second in a big pacing race. Her share of the purse was around thirty thousand. Geoff Dunn had two winners. One was Venus Serena who won the 175,000 feature race. We were delighted as we have been working with all of them, mainly to help get them properly balanced.

THE WARD BROTHERS

When I first began to travel to New Zealand, I stayed at The Commodore Hotel near the airport in Christchurch. Barry Ward was the night manager of the hotel and he also trained standardbred horses, which were my favorite. I grew up with standardbreds and owned a couple of them at the time. Barry and I had something in common – horses. He gave me a very good rate on my room. In exchange, I looked at his horses every night if any of them were having any problems. Sometimes I even worked on his brother Michael's horses that Barry was training.

The Commodore Hotel ended up being my main headquarters. Everyone knew that they could reach me there. After dinner every night I would meet Barry at his office in the hotel and we would go over his horses. This went on for a few years until Barry quit working there. This is where I got to know his brother Michael. Michael was an top notch builder. After the Commodore Hotel was built, he had added a second floor and then another floor and then another. Michael was such a good builder that he built a 13th and 14th story on a downtown office building. A house that I owned in Christchurch was up for sale, it sold and the closing was scheduled for Friday. The tenant in the house called me early on the Friday of the closing to tell me that a pipe had burst in the bathroom and there was damage to the floor and all of the walls were ruined from water damage. I called Michael to tell him about the problem and he said that he would go take a look at it and get back with me. Around noon that day Michael called me back and said, "You can go ahead with the closing. Everything is back together except for the painting" and said that he would do that next week. The buyer said that would be alright.

We helped Michael on a regular basis with his horses. One day, he said that he might need a new well and asked me if I would come over and mark a well site for him. We marked two or three, but the best site ended up one being near the barn. It appeared to be better water quality and a better water flow, so we marked it. I showed Michael and his son Craig how to locate water that day with L-Rods. We couldn't mark the spot with a stake because the horses may hurt themselves and trip over it, so Michael used his Geometry skills and measured from three different fence posts. He wrote down the exact distance between the fence posts and the well site. He carried the measurements inside and put them on the wall of the barn, so that he would not forget where we had marked it. A few years later, he called a well driller to come and drill a well for him. Michael showed them the exact location for the well that I had found and the well drillers told him that they did not think that the spot that I had found was a good well site. Michael told them, "This is the spot that Bill Northern found and this is where you are going to drill for my well."

After the drillers drilled the well, they told Michael, "This is the best well in West Melton!"

DOWSING FOR A WELL

John Barber is a deer farmer who lives near Oxford who needed a new well. His well at the time was not far from the river and when the river is very high, his water gets a bit muddy and tastes a bit different. John, Lester, and John's friend Diane came and collected me a bit before 10 a.m. We rode out to his farm in Oxford stopping along the way to pick up some lunch for later. John took me to the site of the well and showed me where the power line was. He wanted a new well near the power line if possible. I took out a piece of paper and placed it on the hood of the car. Then I marked off the field, the power line, and present well. The field behind the well seemed to be a better place to look for a well site. It was considerably uphill from where we were but the power line ran through it. I was able to locate, on the drawing, three underground veins of pure drinking water, all within 25 meters of the surface.

Next, I gave everyone a set of L-rods and asked them to help me dowse for the best place to drill a new well. We chose a vein of water that seemed to offer the best flow and water quality, It seemed it could even offer some water for irrigation if needed. Once everyone except John had dowsed the best location for a new well, we piled a few stones to mark the location. John, for some reason, seemed a bit frightened of the dowsing rods.

After lunch Diane took Lester over to Lew Driver's to go over some horses and check on the energy. John brought me back to Michael's. Then Michael took me down the road to look at a pacer for a friend of his. We were able to tell his friend some things the horse thought were not right about his training and shoeing. I understand that after the changes were made, the horse improved. Aimee Edmonds rang to say that she, John Dunn, and Robert Dunn were coming the next day for dowsing lessons. Pauline made copies of some horse photos for the class. Michael cooked some steaks on the barbie for dinner.

These are all excellent horse people. John is one of the top ten drivers. Robert, his father, is one of the top trainers, and Aimee's family has been in the business a long time.

A Day of Dowsing Lessons

The dowsing students all arrived around 1 p.m. We got started right away by locating underground things in the yard. They found the water and electric lines. Then they located underground veins of water. Michael arrived while they were looking for water and told them how we had located his well site a few years ago. The well driller wanted to drill in a different location than we had marked, but Michael said he insisted that they drill exactly where we had marked the well to be drilled.   Pauline fixed us some sandwiches for lunch. In the afternoon, we did some map dowsing of my house and lot in Virginia. We then let them go over their property for any negative or noxious energy and underground water. We then turned to going over horses and this is where the fun began as there was a bit of arguing about where the horses we gave them were sore. I was called on to be the arbitrator. Everyone left feeling good about their ability to dowse their horses. I hope this new skill will bring them great success in their work.

Testimonial

Dear Bill,

Every one here is well including the horses. We are only too pleased to describe our experiences from your visit to New Zealand for your book and are happy for our names to be included if you wish. We feel it was an extremely fulfilling experience to have the opportunity to meet you, attend your dowsing course and learn so many other skills which we would not have associated with dowsing.

Joyce's Story

Earlier this year Bill came to cleanse my property and put a protective light around it to rid the house of negative energy. He also gave me the skills to protect myself against negative energy in my job as a Community Psychiatric Nurse. After a very hot dry period, the well on our property dried up the day before Bill arrived. He dowsed to find another underground stream. The one he found was 20 feet lower than the original and would need to be moved across in an arc about five feet to be in line with the well. This I thought would be an impossible feat and my husband was extremely skeptical as he has a scientific mind. Bill, however, was in no doubt that this was possible, and with his powers and dowsing skills we had water flowing at full force within three days and still there had been no rain. Needless to say my husband was somewhat speechless.

Thank you, Bill.

Regards, Joyce Campion (New Zealand)

KEN WINS BIG AS A FILL-IN JOCKEY

I went to the Mobil station to wait for Michael, Pauline and Craig to collect me around noon, to go to the races in Ashburton. Their best horse, Majestic Time was racing in a featured race. At the time, she was probably the best three-year-old trotting filly in New Zealand. She was racing in about a $90,000 stake race with the colts. I think New Zealand is the only country where the fillies have to race with the colts. She was in with 17 other colts and fillies. She drew a post position in the middle of the front line. Her regular driver Ken Barron was in Australia racing some of his horses but they were not going very well. When he found out Majestic Time was in the big race, he rang Michael and asked it he could come drive her. Michael had promised the drive to another driver as Ken was away. However, when Michael told the other driver that Ken had called and wanted to fly back to drive her, the other driver said he understood the situation. We passed by Geoff Dunn's good horse on the way into the stalls and the groom told us she had won her race and set a new track record. I told him Geoff would give him a nice bonus for that. He held up his sandwich and said, "He has already given it to me."

Majestic Time's race called the "Hambletonian" went off, and Ken took her back to the middle of the field, parked out second from the rail all the way. When the horses reached the top of the stretch, Ken took her out three wide and was passing horses down the stretch, almost like she had wings. She won by a length ahead of the nearest colt. She set another track record for three year old filly trotters. I was so happy tears were flowing from my face. It had only been a few weeks since we were called to see if we could get her going back to last years form and now she is setting track records. We were working with two horses that set new track records today.

This is a great day for me and my Angels.

DOWSING FOR A LOST PILOT

In January of 1998 when I arrived at the Burrowes' house in Rakaia, New Zealand, I was told someone was waiting to see me. He had evidently been waiting a couple of hours over at the garage and thought it was very important for me to see him this afternoon. I put my suitcases in the house and went over to the garage. The man was Don Edgar, a friend of a family who had lost an airplane pilot. It seems that just a few weeks ago this pilot had left Greymouth on the West Coast in his small plane with a load of Whitebait. Whitebait is a Kiwi delicacy available seasonally; tiny fish about half the size of minnows we fish with. The are prepared in many ways but probably the most popular use for them is being cooked in an omelet.

Mr. Edgar told me his story of how the pilot and plane had gone missing somewhere between Greymouth and Christchurch. He had some of the pilot's personal belongings and an aerial map of the area. He was familiar with dowsing and in fact was a good dowser himself. There are many ways to map dowse and he had been told we were good at map dowsing by one of our students. We spread out the map and I went over it with a long straight edge up, and then across. I told him where the lines cross on the map is where the missing plane and pilot should be. Tyrone Burrowes was there and since I had taught him the previous year, I enlisted his aid to go over the map a second time. This time, I had Tyrone slide the straight edge. I turned my back and, watching my pendulum swing, told Tyrone when to stop the straight edge. He then marked the map in both directions. The place where the two lines crossed this time was within a half inch of where they crossed on the first try.

Don did not think this was the right place and showed me the method he used to map dowse. He found them in a different location than we did. We later learned that Don took this map to the New Zealand Air Force who had been searching for the plane. He was told that the spot we marked could well have been on his flight path that day because of some bad weather. They said if the plane did go down in that area it was highly unlikely to ever be found as this was rough mountainous country. I did not hear from Don again until arriving in Rakaia at the same place in 1999.

Don and Lester Take Lessons From Bill

This time he had left an urgent message for me to ring him as soon as I arrived. I caught up with some friends around the garage and jam factory before ringing him. I rang him around 5 p.m. and he told me that he now lived near Alexandria, a four and a half hour drive. He and a friend, Lester Morris, a breeder of thoroughbreds, needed to come up and take dowsing lessons from me. The reason they were taking lessons from me was because they had dowsed for and marked a well site on Lester's farm in Central Otago and yet they found no water there.

They arrived Friday morning and I went over some of the basics of dowsing with them even though they could both dowse. Lester could use the standard dowsing tools but Don liked to cup his hands as though he was holding a butterfly and hold them out in front of him until he got a reaction of the hands being pulled downward. Map dowsing is usually the last thing we cover for the day and again Don insisted on showing me how he did it. He carried a pendulum around in a little bottle of spring water. He did not want it contaminated by anyone's hands or pocket dirt. They had brought a survey plat of Lester's farm and we used that as one of our projects to find water. They both marked a place on the map but decided to go with the location we marked. They later drilled on this spot and found the amount of water we thought was there.

Lester Morris was the most gifted student with animals that I had ever had the privilege to teach. By the end of our map dowsing session, he could put his hand on a drawing of a horse and tell everything that was wrong with the horse as well as what the horse liked to do. Lester had two horses racing at Riccarton Race Course in Christchurch the following day. I decided to go.

I saw Lester almost as soon as I got to the track. He was looking at the program going over each horse to see how they felt. He told a friend he had driven up yesterday to take dowsing lessons. The friend said he now knew for sure that Lester was getting soft in the head. Lester told him it was the best four hours he had ever spent in is life.

THE HORSE WHO WAS PICKY ABOUT COLORS

There was a horse that had been racing well and was then sold to someone else, but it still stayed in the same barn with the same trainer. He was bringing home a check almost every start. His jockey wore bold red colors. After the sale, the horse wasn't racing well at all and the trainer couldn't figure out why. She contacted me to see if we could figure out why this horse all of a sudden didn't want to race. After listening to him, he told me that one of the problems was *those new sissy colors that my jockey wears.* Light blue. He also told me that he didn't like the new color of her hair that she had just dyed the night before. He was also sore in a few places, but not sore enough to race poorly. When I told her what the horse had shared with me, she said, "I only dyed my hair one shade different than what it was, he shouldn't have even noticed! I will dye it back to the shade that it was." From the trainer's point of view, in order for the owner to switch colors, they have to go to the stewards and get approval. They have to have designs and it is not easy because it has to be approved by the entire racing commission. They gave her permission to change the colors for one race, just to see if it made a difference. The horse started and won the race easily. The permission was granted to change the colors for good.

J. EWING'S ORGANIC FERTILIZER

One day my friend Alistar, who lived in Papatoetoe, New Zealand, told me about a man name J. Ewing that produced organic fertilizer from minerals from the ocean mixed with rocks from the mountains. He pulverized them and made the fertilizer. Alister decided to take me to see this gentleman and I was a little skeptical at first. We drove around 30 minutes to Mr. Ewing's farm and he began to tell us all about the crops that he had grown and was still growing, using this special fertilizer. He was selling the product, mainly on the South Island, but also on the North Island where he produced the fertilizer as well. The South Island heard about it and they were "ready to give it a go!" It took the North Island a while to come around. He shipped it by either trucks or ships for the really large orders. I can remember observing some of the fields all over New Zealand and at times, I took notice that some of the crops were much greener and healthier than others. When I inquired about what they were using, the answer was always the same, "A special fertilizer from up north and it only needs to be applied once every 3-4 years."

Mr. Ewing showed us one tomato that he had grown and two tomatoes that he had purchased from the grocery store. He had three paper cups and he put all three tomatoes under paper cups and moved them around so that there was no way that we could tell which tomato was under which cup. Alister and I both were always able to pick up on which one was grown on Mr. Ewing's property because of the greater energy that the tomato had versus the other two. One of us used dowsing rods and the other used a pendulum, we never missed which one was his tomato. We talked for a long time and he invited us to stay for dinner. He had been telling us about the cattle that he raised and that he was selling the meat to Japan because it was very near the flavor and texture of Kobe Beef, which is very expensive. The difference between Mr. Ewing's beef and other farmers' beef was that he had his cattle grazing in fields treated with his organic fertilizer and the others did not. Mr. Ewing served all of us roast beef at dinner and it was amazing how much flavor the beef had and how tender it was. There was definitely a huge difference. I was fascinated.

There was a fella there from South Africa that had a calculator that was made like one of the radionics machines with a witness plate. When we would put one of the crops from the Ewing Farm on the plate, he would get a reading of the correct number of the product's energy from this calculator. This still amazes me. The big fertilizer companies kept suing Mr. Ewing because he was calling his product fertilizer. Finally, his legal expenses piled up so high, he went out of business.

THE INVISIBLE ARBORIST FROM DUNEDIN

I was flying nine hours from New Zealand to Hawaii and the passenger next to me was the Arborist from Dunedin. We began talking and I found out that he was a wine connoisseur. So I let him order the wine for both of us. He told me what he did for a living and then it was my turn. He had a hard time believing it, as do most people. I told him about a French coil, which is a process of wrapping wire around a tree to keep it healthy. I also told him about Bob Crowder, a well known Organic Expert in New Zealand who was head of the Organic Department at Lincoln University and well known for his knowledge of raising all plants without the use of chemicals. I shared with my co-passenger that I had taught Bob about how to use a French coil and the results were memorable. More wine was served and then I told him all about energy fields. I explained to him that you can make yourself invisible, if you want to, by bringing in energy to your body, so that people don't feel it or see you. As we had another glass of wine, he thought that he could see how this might work. I noticed that the flight attendants were serving lunch, but we were having so much fun talking and having wine that we didn't pay much attention to them. Shortly, the main flight attendant came by an asked us if we would like some dessert. I told her, "We would like to have some lunch first!"

She looked at me like I had lost my mind. She asked the other flight attendants why we didn't get lunch. They responded, "We didn't see them, they must have moved up here from the Coach section."

The main flight attendant retrieved the seating chart and confirmed our correct seats. Obviously, we had not moved from the Coach section; they just didn't see us! We were served lunch and my new friend almost became a believer! When he returned to New Zealand, he wrote about French coils and how they can make trees healthier.

LEAVING NEW ZEALAND

On one of our first trips to New Zealand, we had been visiting Roydon Lodge and Fred Fletcher and were spending a lot of time with both. We were scheduled to fly out of Christchurch one morning and Maury, Ruth, Fred and Faye Fletcher and a few others came to see us off to the airport before we left for home. We were all in a tea shop and were chatting away and this lady said, "You are really a nice fellow to have so many friends come to see you off!"

Maury spoke up. "We just want to make sure that he gets on the damn plane!"

TAKING STOCK
OF A GREAT TRIP

This has been probably the most rewarding visit in the 23 years I have been going to New Zealand. Not financially rewarding but by the accomplishments we had a part of. I got to work with some great people, animals, trainers and farriers. Most of all was having the opportunity to live with the Ward family for two weeks. It is unbelievable how hard they work and all work together. They go out of their way to help others, and when they needed a hand putting up the oats, neighbors showed up to help them. It was just like it's supposed to be and how it *was* years ago here in the U.S.

Tyrone was taking a flight to Auckland so I joined him and another man for a bit of breakfast in the lounge operated by Air New Zealand. They have nice lounges in Auckland and Christchurch. I took this opportunity to thank Tyrone for his help during my stay and to return his cell phone. Then I walked over to the international terminal for my flight to

Honolulu. Tyrone had informed me of a gate for business class passengers that let you go through security fairly quickly. The Kiwis don't think of every passenger as a threat the way we do here. The plane was the same old plane I flew down on.

The man in the seat next to me was familiar with the New Zealand Society of Dowsing. He was not frightened to talk about dowsing so he told me about some of his experiences. It seems he has some negative energy in one of his houses. I did a drawing of the house and told him the problem was where the streams crossed under the house. The place where they crossed was where he spent a few hours every evening. I explained to him how to shift the streams and how to neutralize the energy.

130

Clerk of the Course

MY WINE-MAKING, HARNESS RACING FRIEND, DOC MACDONALD

While I was managing the Howard Johnson's Restaurant in Maryland on the corner of University Boulevard and Riggs Road, I found out that further down University Boulevard, a fella had ponies that he brought out every afternoon for children to ride. His name was Mr. Wiseman and he only charged 25 cents per pony ride. Each 25-cent ride didn't last for very long, maybe five minutes. My daughter, Debbie, really enjoyed riding the ponies. I would usually give him a few dollars and tell Mr. Wiseman to let Debbie ride the pony until she got tired.

There was another older gentleman there who enjoyed watching the children ride the ponies. His name was Angus MacDonald, but everyone called him "Doc." Doc sort of took a liking to me, I guess because of the fact that I always gave Mr. Wiseman a few dollars for Debbie to ride all that she wanted.

Doc struck up a conversation with me one night and I found out that he was a retired veterinarian. He had previously been the head of the Veterinary Department at the University of Maryland. Through talking to him, I discovered that he had a love for harness horses and I had the same fondness for them. Unfortunately, Doc's wife did not like horses and she wouldn't let him own one. Doc got the idea that he would buy his son a farm up in Frederick, Maryland, with the thought in the back of his mind that he could go up there and buy a couple of horses and his son would help him train them. Unfortunately, Doc's son's wife didn't like horses either and would not allow any horses on their farm. It was basically the same as a cattle farm, she just didn't want any horses.

Meeting The Ontario Swindler

But Doc insisted on having a horse of his own. He had a friend named Charlie Finn that had inherited a farm with some horses. Charlie didn't know what to do with the horses and he decided to sell a horse, jog cart, and harness for 300. Doc couldn't have horses of his own because of his wife, so he talked me into buying it. We were going to be partners, he said. "Just don't tell my wife!"

I brought the horse to Warsaw to have my friend, Garland King, train it. During breaking one day, the horse reared up and fell backwards on its tail and broke it. After Garland got the horse going, he sent it up to me at Rosecroft Raceway. I would wake up at 4 o'clock in the morning to go over to Rosecroft and jog the horse for a couple of hours. There were some very friendly trainers at Rosecroft who would give me a hand because this horse liked to run away from me. I would get into the cart and have someone else check her head up. As soon as her head was checked up, she took off, with me just steering. Several times, she took me through the guardrail and threw me to the ground.

I didn't know a whole lot about horses at the time, it was all new to me. If it hadn't been for the Rosecroft trainers helping me, I don't know what I would have done. I couldn't do it all by myself. After a few months, one of my friends that was a Rosecroft Sidewheeler had a brother just outside of London,

Ontario, that wanted to buy the mare. So I agreed to sell her to him. His brother came to my work at Howard Johnson's to get me to sign the papers so he could take the horse across the border. He didn't have the money for the horse, so I agreed that he could pay me the following week because I had already known him from the Sidewheelers. I trusted him.

But he didn't pay me. My wife, Ann, and I notified the man that we were coming to London, Ontario, to collect my money. We drove to to where he was at the training track in London jogging some horses. He invited us to come into his trailer and have a cup of tea. The white teacups were very dirty on the inside and the place was full of flies everywhere flying all over the place. Neither Ann nor myself, could drink the tea. We finally asked him for the money for the horse and he said, "I can't pay you today, but I will send you a check next week."

He never did send me a check for the horse and, at that time, I needed the money. The sad part of the story is that the mare never did win a race. She also had between 6-7 foals and none of them ever won a race either.

That is what happens to you when you screw Bill Northern.

Making Wine with Doc in Giant Drums

Doc had a good friend named Milt Taylor who was the presiding judge in Maryland. Doc told Milt that I would be a good judge, so when Baltimore Raceway opened up that year, Milt hired me as a judge.

Doc liked to drink wine and make wine. His wife was a strict Southern Baptist and wouldn't let him bring the wine into the house. I lived in an apartment at the time and we would make the wine there. I sold vegetables to restaurants and there was always leftover produce. We made wine in 20 gallon drums. Sometimes we would have two drums working at the same time. We made wine out of dandelions, peaches, grapes and even potatoes. Doc had the bottles, he took care of cleaning them, putting the stoppers in, straining the wine through the cheesecloth, etc. He would take the bottles of wine home and hide them in the garage so that his wife couldn't find them. Our friendship lasted a long time. From meeting him, getting the job as a judge at the racetrack and making wine together, we always had fun. I used to visit Doc frequently, he lived right there on University Boulevard.

One day I went to visit him and he was sitting on his front porch. I noticed that the left side of his jaw was protruding out and I asked him what the problem was. He said, "I have a bad tooth." I asked him why he wouldn't go to the dentist and he said, "I did go, but he wanted 10 to pull it."

His Scotch heritage kept him from just paying the 10 to get the tooth pulled. I returned the next week to visit him and his jaw was sticking out even further and I said, "Doc, you've got to do something about that tooth!"

He said, "I did! I pulled it out myself with horse forceps!" I asked why it was still swollen.

"I pulled the wrong tooth!"

CLEANING OYSTER HOUSES & THE USDA

When I had Wardico, Inc. I took the oyster house business very seriously. I tried to look out for them, just like all of the other customers. I tried to sell them what was best for their business, I wasn't just concerned with Wardico's profit. I treated them the way that I would want to be treated. Oyster houses had inspections once per month and they had to make sure that everything was spotless. They were using detergents to clean with and, as a sanitizer, they were using calcium hypochlorite. This particular sanitizer did an excellent job of killing germs and worked perfectly. One of the inspectors thought that putting this effluent back into the creek was causing a problem for the fish and wildlife. He did not realize that it dissipated in warm water and once in the creek within a matter of a few hours, it was gone. This is what most municipalities use to treat their water with today. The inspector decided that they should all use iodine as a sanitizer.

Iodine is a good sanitizer, but it discolors everything. His idea was that if they used iodine, then when he looked up at the walls to see if they were clean, he could tell easier whether the sanitizer had been used or not. The oyster house owners were complaining to me because the iodine was a lot more expensive and as far as they were concerned, it didn't work any better than the calcium hypochlorite. We tried to reason with the inspector with no luck, so I wrote to my two senators and my congressman. I told them the situation. They in turn got the USDA involved and decided that the calcium hypochlorite was fine and that there was no need to use iodine. This is a perfect example of being sure to use your congressman when you have a problem with the federal government. The inspector is now my congressman.

MOTHER'S DEPRESSION
& THE EXORCISM

I had heard about a Dowser's Convention that was being held in Vermont and I was quite excited to go. My mother was living in the house where I am living now, by herself and had become very depressed. So depressed that she had not left the house in three months. She loved to bake cakes, so she baked cakes often for everyone. If you were sick, she baked a cake for you. Her friends would run to the grocery store for her and she would bake cakes for them, too. I was hesitant to go to this convention in Vermont because I wasn't sure if I should leave her at home alone or not.

But I decided to go. My wife and I flew to Vermont and drove to Lyndonville where the convention was being held. We both took a lot of classes and we were very impressed with all of the things that could be done with dowsing. Previously, we'd had no idea.

During the course of the week, I took a course on

exorcism taught by John Van Drie. I sat next to Dick Paskowski and we were told to think of somebody that had a problem. Put the name on a piece of paper and give the paper to the person next to us. Dick gave me the name of a person who was an alcoholic. I gave Dick my mother's name. John was instructing us on what to do and I was following his directions. I looked over at Dick and he had perspiration running down his face. I asked him if he was alright. He said, "This woman has a wall of concrete around her. I think that I have broken it all up."

The class ended and we all discussed who we had been working with. There were varying degrees of success and I wasn't very sure if the person that I was working on had gotten better or not. Dick was pretty sure that he had been successful with my mother. He had already had some experience with this and he was experienced in taking care of negative and noxious energy fields.

We flew home on a Sunday and on Monday morning I tried to call my mother, but got no answer. So I called the person that was checking on her for me and she didn't know

where she was either.

It turns out that she was at the grocery store shopping

for the very first time in months. She had been seeing a

psychiatrist in Richmond for months. She had an appointment

with him soon after we returned from Vermont. I took her to

her appointment in Richmond and after talking to her, the

nurse said that the doctor would like to talk to me. I thought

maybe he thought I was crazy too! Amazed by her progress,

the doctor sat me down and looked at me just as serious and

said, "What in the hell has happened with this woman?"

I told him about the the exorcism class and how it

worked and he was amazed. He told me that he had read about

it but this was the first time that he had ever seen it for

himself. It was great to see my mother back to her old self

again. Every now and then I could see that she was going back

into a depression and I would have Dick get her straight. From

then on, Dick the person that I used to call on if I needed for

someone to be cleared.

CHRISPIN & A WORLD OF NEW CONNECTIONS

While I was living in Lexington, Kentucky in 2008, I was called out to Hurricane Run Farm to see some horses. As I can recall, there were around four horses for us to see when we got there. They had various problems that we were able to pinpoint. I communicated with some of the horses and they told me that they didn't even want to be a racehorse. One of the horses belonged to Chrispin, a young lady around 30 years old. Chrispin had been taking lame race horses to her farm from the racetrack trying to nurture them back to good health. She used anything that she needed -- chiropractors, farriers, people like myself, whatever it took. We didn't get to communicate with Chrispin that day, but the groom told her everything that we had said. She was very impressed that we could find these problems which had been bugging her.

A few days later, Chrispin called me out to the farm where she kept her horses. She had another horse for us to take a look at. We went over the horse for her and pointed the

problem. She wound up introducing me to many people that

she worked for. Among them were Hugo Murray, a worldly

livestock broker, John Stuart, a successful horse consigner,

and Andrew, a fellow from New York who was in the ladies

fashion business that usually spent at least 1 million dollars

per year on buying horses.

Looking Over Yearlings at Keeneland

My first encounter with these fellows occurred while

we were at the September Yearling Sale at Keeneland, which

is a 14-day sale wherein the first 3-4 days they present the

most expensive yearlings.

I was walking around with Hugo, who had his list of

yearlings that he wanted to see. Since I was with him,

whenever they brought out a yearling, I would take a look at it

too. Hugo was an excellent horseman, so he picked up on a lot

of problems with these yearlings very easily. While I was there,

I was asking the animals if they had any lameness issues and if they wanted to be a racehorse. At this time, Hugo was not a full believer, but he was open-minded. Hugo and I spent the entire day going over yearlings.

On the second day, Hugo was beginning to think that maybe I had something going on! He was paying more attention to what I said that I had picked up on these yearlings. Before the day was over, he was convinced that what I was doing was beneficial, to the point to where when I told him that a yearling didn't want to be a racehorse, he didn't bid on it.

A year later, he even paid for Ann and I to come to his mansion in Ireland to teach him and his daughters how to dowse. Whenever Hugo invited us to Ireland, we never had to spend one single dollar for anything. He even took us to the races and gave us Irish money to bet with. He covered it all and it was completely unexpected but appreciated.

Dowsing cannot be done rushed or on the spur of the moment, you must be relaxed and ready to listen. I told Hugo this, but he waited until the last minute for us to go over his horses. This was not all his fault, because it rained almost every day that we were there. When you are around Hugo, there isn't really any quiet time because his phone is constantly ringing. We did the best that we could under the circumstances and we told him which yearlings wanted to be a racehorse and which ones didn't.

From Ireland to England

After we finished up with Hugo in Ireland, he took us to the airport and we flew over to England and visited Avesbury and Stonehenge. When in Avesbury, if you are walking around with your dowsing rods, everyone asks, "Have you found anything interesting?" Whereas here, if you were to walk around with dowsing rods in your hands, people would think that you were crazy! I found almost all of the lay lines that were in the area. From there we flew home.

Return to Keeneland

The next year, at the yearling sale, we were working for Michael Lehy and some of his horses. We went to the track kitchen to have lunch. While we were eating lunch, I noticed that a couple of people were from Ireland by their accent. When Michael left, I went over and chatted with them, not having any idea of who they were. I told them that I had been to Ireland with Hugo and had greatly enjoyed it and then told them a little bit about what I did. They were nice, but didn't believe a thing I told them, though they listened. Later on I ran into Hugo and he told me that they had asked him about me. He told them that it was for real! It turns out that these two men that I was talking to, one was the president of Coolmore, the largest thoroughbred breeder in the world, and the other was a partner with them in many horses. Since they had been talking to Hugo, Mr. Magner came up to me at the sale the next day and took me aside and asked if I could go over a horse for him in Ireland. I told him I could, but I needed a picture of the horse and where it was located. He told me that he would have to go out to his farm in Lexington and get a picture and bring it to me the next day.

Meeting the Thoroughbred, Montjeu

The next day at the sale, he brought a picture of Montjeu to me. This horse is the highest rated horse ever by Saber's Wells and one of the best young sires in the world. We went to a quiet place so that I could take a took a look at the horse's picture. I asked him what the problem was and he said that the horse had stopped breeding mares. The horse told me that the reason that he wasn't breeding mares was because one of the mares kicked him. Mr. Magner didn't think that a mare could have possibly kicked Montjeu. I asked again and Montjeu told me, "He did *too* kick me!"

A few weeks after the sale was over, the Office Manager at Coolmore called me and asked, "Mr. Northern, when would it be convenient and how soon could you you get on a plane and fly to Ireland?"

I had no idea who or what Coolmore was. I wanted to teach someone, so I told them that I should bring my wife and we could teach dowsing while we were there. In a few days,

Ann and I arrived in Ireland and were picked up at the airport by one of Coolmore's four drivers. Since we had been flying all night, they escorted us directly to our hotel so that we could rest and then we would go to the farm and go to work.

Arriving at Coolmore

When we arrived at Coolmore, we were introduced to the three people that we were going to teach as well as the office staff. We started with these three people by giving them an introduction to dowsing, then after we practiced for a little while, I turned them over to Ann.

Montjeu was in a paddock all by himself. The fence consisted of shrubbery that was at least five feet thick so that he couldn't get out. The only way to enter the paddock was through a gate. They showed me where he was and brought me a chair to sit on by the gate to Montjeu's paddock. Montjeu's stud fee was 130,000 euro and no one was allowed to enter his paddock, that is how valuable this horse was. The first day, I sat with him for over two hours and I wasn't able to convince him that he should go back to breeding again. He wouldn't even consider it. They showed me around the farm a little bit and then I caught up with Ann and the students and worked with them for a little while. On the second day, we began working with the dowsing students because they had jobs to do and they didn't have the entire day to spend on dowsing. The people at Coolmore were aware that I could dowse but did not have enough confidence in the students. One day we were using the bronze statue of Sadler's Wells as a representation for another horse we were attempting to find out where he hurt. When teaching animal communication, I usually give the students a horse that I have already gone over and then have them go over it and see what they can find. I then tell them what I found.

Mr. Magner came along and asked what we were doing. We told him and he just walked away. It was quite comical. We continued on. That afternoon I went back to sitting with Montjeu.

On the third day, since I had gotten a little hungry on the first two days while sitting and communicating with

Montjeu, I asked the driver to stop by the greengrocer. I purchased three apples for my snack. I arrived at Coolmore and was greeted by the workers. They showed me to Montjeu's paddock and I began to sit there in my chair again attempting to get him to listen to me. No luck. Finally, after a while, I was hungry and took one of my apples out of my bag, took a bite and Montjeu came over to the gate and said, *I think that I would like to try that.*

So I gave him a bite of my apple and he really liked it. Then he wanted another bite. I just gave him the rest of the apple. Later on, I wanted another apple, so I took another one out and began to eat it. Over comes Montjeu again. So I gave him the rest of that apple, too. He said, *You know, I think that I would start doing it again if they would give me one of these every time!*

I asked him, "Montjeu, if I give you my last apple would you start doing it again?"

He said *Yes,* and we had a deal!

Montjeu ended up keeping his end of the bargain and

began to breed again. I was told that after that, Coolmore made over 40 million euros, once Montjeu started breeding again.

The next day we went to Ballydoyle, Coolmore's Training Center, and were quite impressed with the different tracks that they had for the horses. They had a very large crew just to care for each track. We were asked to go over to David's farm, who was Mr. Magner's son-in-law, and mark a well site for him. When we saw him at the sale in Lexington the following year, he said that it ended up being a very good well for him. We didn't get to meet Aidan O'Brien, the head trainer, which was a disappointment. He is probably the best horse trainer in the world.

Leveling with Hurricane Run

When I arrived from the hotel, they had everything ready for Hurricane Run, who was a very picky stallion. There were some mares that he just didn't care for and if he didn't like them, he would not breed them, and that was it.

In Ireland, the Gypsy horses are tied out by the road to graze because they usually don't have a farm to graze on. On this particular morning, Hurricane Run just wouldn't breed. So we took a break for lunch and after that I decided to take a nap on one of the nice leather sofas that were there. I contacted Hurricane Run and told him that if he didn't breed that mare this afternoon, I was going to tie him out with the Gypsy horses! When the time came after lunch, we brought the mare to him he sniffed her once and then took care of business. This was the fastest he had ever bred a mare. Mr. Magner came over and said, "Bill, I can hardly believe it. What did you tell Hurricane Run?"

I told Mr. Magner that I had told him that I was going to put him out with the Gypsy horses if he didn't cooperate this afternoon. Also, that afternoon I discovered that Hurricane Run was sore in his back and that they should have a chiropractor come and take a look at him. So a female chiropractor arrived and he wouldn't allow her to pick his legs up. As you know, manipulation by a chiropractor involves leg movement and Hurricane Run was not going to have it. They drove me back to the hotel that afternoon and when I entered the room, it was very cold in there. I called the front desk and they told me that they didn't ever turn the heat on in the rooms until 6 o'clock, but that I was welcome to come to the lobby and rest by the fireplace until the heat was turned on in my room. Four of the guys that I was working with joined me for dinner. Since they worked for Coolmore, it was a chance for them to eat for free. As I recall, they drank at least four bottles of wine, we were having a good time, and my Coolmore expense account paid for all of it. When they brought out the menu, I was dowsing the different dishes available with my pendulum, of course. The guys jokingly asked, "Bill, what are you doing?"

And I told them that I was asking my angels what I should eat. They snickered and asked what I was going to order, I said, "I know that I'm not ordering the Pork Roast, I'm getting a *big* no on that one."

So one of the guys ordered the pork anyway. It turned

out he developed food poisoning and was out of work for four days! This story is still being told around Ireland.

Waking Up to a Message

Animals often wake me up at night while I am trying to sleep. Hurricane Run woke me up around 2 o'clock in the morning and told me that he wasn't going to breed for me the next day, *Because you got this lady to come in and try to hurt my legs!*

So when the driver picked me up the next morning, I told him what the horse had told me. Sure enough, he wouldn't breed the mare for us that morning. When we got to the farm we went straight to the breeding shed and they brought in Hurricane Run. He did exactly as he had told me when he woke me up the night before, that he wasn't going to breed the mare. And he didn't.

We broke for lunch and I decided to take a nap on one of the nice, long leather sofas near the dining room. While resting, I contacted Hurricane Run and told him that if he didn't breed this mare this afternoon that I was going to tie him beside the road with the Gypsy horses. The low end of the rank for a horse, status wise! That afternoon he walked into the breeding shed and bred the mare right away. Mr. Magner was watching and he came over to me and said, "What in the world did you say to him, Bill?"

And I told him, "I told him that if he didn't breed this afternoon that I was going to put him out with the Gypsy horses."

Mr. Magner just shook his head and walked away. That was all she wrote for Hurricane Run. They sold him to a German buyer shortly after this.

Testimonial

June 14

Dear Mr. Northern,

Decker is doing fabulously well. His coat is beautiful, he has gained weight, and is eating well, possibly too well. I have been riding him around the farm.

I pulled blood today and his calcium was within normal limits! I told him before I drew it, "If it is within normal limits, we will start taking field trips again."

I am much better as well. I am healing my life, and trying to learn that what is to be, is to be; and fretting and making myself miserable will not change the outcome. I am learning to believe the horse, not the lab work, and I think Decker and I are communicating better. I have also removed my self from a lot of drama. My life is good, very good.

Thank you so much for all your help,

Barbara

FINDING INFO LEAK
FOR ANDREW

Andrew was another fellow that was introduced to me by Chrispin. He always came to the September Keeneland Sale and spent roughly 1 million for one yearling. He would have Hugo select his yearlings and ask me to go along, too. There are times that a horse might look really good, but he tells me that he doesn't want to be a racehorse. We have learned not to buy yearlings that do not want to race. One day, Andrew and I were sitting alone in the lounge and Andrew said to me, "Bill, if you can tell which yearlings do not want to be racehorses, could you tell me who is leaking my designs to my competitors?"

I told Andrew that I would try, so I closed my eyes and I looked into his office and I saw a woman that I suspected of selling his secrets. I also saw that this woman wasn't particularly selling his designs, rather, she was giving them away to her lover. After I saw this, I was able to describe her to

Andrew so that he knew exactly who I was talking about. I didn't hear anymore about it, but a week later, I received a nice check in the mail from him.

WE SENT THE PRICEY WATER SELLERS PACKING

I was attending the Southwest Dowsing Conference in Flagstaff, Arizona, and there were vendors, all of which were speakers. In order to be a vendor, you must also be a speaker. Most vendors had bottled water for sale, but a particular husband and wife team were selling "special" water. They were saying that the University of California had come up with a way to make this particular water very healthy. They were selling it as "Water With Health Benefits" with a high markup. I was curious, so I decided to set up an experiment. We took samples of water from both bottled water vendors (the "healthy" water and the regular distilled bottled water), tap water, and water from the filtered water fountain. There were four of us, Raymond Grace, Susan Collins, Tony Gehringer, and myself. Each of us had four cups, each one containing a sample of each type of water. We had put labels on the bottom of the cups so we didn't know which water was in which cup. We did this experiment in the open hallway and we drew a crowd of people that wanted to see what we were doing. All four of us dowsed our four cups of water, using our pendulums, and asking the same question, "Which one of these cups of water is the healthiest?"

All four of us either selected the filtered water straight from the water fountain, or the regular tap water. None of us got that either of bottled waters were healthy. It wasn't long after this experiment that the husband and wife team packed up and left.

DOWSING UTILITY LINES FOR THE CREW IN FLAGSTAFF

We were staying at the Americana Hotel for the Southwest Dowsing Conference in Flagstaff, Arizona. We liked to go into town for lunch. On this particular day, we noticed they were about to pave the parking lot. Some of the workers were looking for something and they appeared to be getting frustrated. I stopped and asked. They were repaving the lot and they had located all of the wires running to all of the light poles except for one. They couldn't risk tearing one of the wires up, so they had to find it.

I went to the car and got my L-rods. I found the line immediately using my rods and I marked where the wire was underground, where it came from and where it went to. The workers were quite skeptical and began to carefully dig to see if that was where the wire was. They saw I was correct and asked, "Where can we get tools like those?"

Six of them went into the Vendor area of the Conference and purchased L-rods. When they came out with them, I showed them how to use them.

THE HORSE THAT WOULDN'T DRINK WATER IN HIS PADDOCK

I was called to a horse farm near Charlottesville, Virginia, because there was a horse that was not drinking his water in his paddock. I went over the horse and he seemed to be somewhat dehydrated. When I took him into the stall, he drank the water from the bucket. So I led him back into the paddock and noticed that before he got up to his water, he hesitated for a minute. That is when I realized that there was an energy line that the horse did not want to cross. I took out my dowsing rods and found that there was a negative energy line there and that was why the horse did not want to cross it, even to drink his water. I asked my angels to please change the energy to beneficial energy and what was strange was that the horse still thought that the energy line was there. Once I showed him that it was gone, he was fine and drank water again in his paddock.

CALMING A HORSE AT COLONIAL DOWNS

One day when I arrived at the Colonial Downs Racetrack, I received a message from the State Veterinarian to contact him when I came onto the grounds. They had a horse that was really acting crazy in one of the stalls. As soon as I contacted the vet, he told me where the horse was located and I immediately went to see him. It turned out that there was a negative energy line running right through the middle of the stall. Some animals can handle this, but obviously this horse was not able to deal with it. The horse was rearing up, didn't want anyone to enter the stall, and was very unhappy. I asked my angels to please change the energy line to positive energy. Almost immediately, the horse calmed down. This vet had seen what we could do in the past and had become a believer. He said that he had never seen anything like this before.

APPEARING ON TV AGAIN: *RIPLEY'S BELIEVE IT OR NOT*

The folks at *Ripley's Believe It Or Not* somehow got my name and contacted me regarding doing a segment on animal communication with me. They sent a contract to me and my attorney looked over it and made a couple of changes, which they agreed to. We decided to meet with them at Colonial Downs Race Track in New Kent County. This was the first pari-mutuel race track in Virginia. The racing secretary then contacted a few top notch trainers and all but one of them declined. So we had one of the top ten trainers who I had worked with before, and one regular trainer that I wasn't familiar with. We worked with the horse of the well-known trainer first and, of course, the producer called all of the shots. They instructed us on where to stand in order to get the best picture for the camera. All of this was taking place in a 12 x 12 stall. I went over the first horse for the top ten trainer and he told me where he was hurting, what he liked to do, the jockey that he would like to ride him and how far that he wanted the race to go, etc. Then the producer met with the trainer, away from where I was, and asked him questions about my readings and whether or not I was accurate. Then they brought in the trainer I was unfamiliar with and we did the same thing with his horse. This trainer was very skeptical of me and what we were doing right from the start. It was very obvious that he was having a hard time believing that we could see and hear these things that only he knew about his horse. When the producer met with him, away from me, he said to them, "I still don't know about that guy. I think that he's reading my mind, not the horses!"

My thought was, what would made him think that if I could read his mind that I couldn't read the horse's mind?

It had been a few months and I had not heard from them. When I contacted them their response was that the people at Sony, the owners of *Ripley's Believe It Or Not* at the time, were having a tough time believing that someone could do what we could do. The producer told me that he almost had the folks at Sony believing that this was for real and that it shouldn't be much longer before the show would air.

I was in New Zealand when they contacted me to tell me that my segment was about to air. So I didn't get to see it, of course, but someone taped it for me. I was quite disappointed when my segment lasted only a couple of minutes.

THE HORSE WHO WATCHED THE CLOCK

I was working at the Culpeper Horse Show in Virginia where a well-known Grand Prix rider and his wife Jackie were showing their horses. Jackie was trying to convert a Grand Prix horse, which is a jumper event, into a hunter horse, which focuses on style and less objective measures. In the Grand Prix jumping divisions, horses are timed, and every second counts. If the horse is the least bit slow and it takes longer that is should for him to go the course, that would result in a time fault. Each second is a time fault which means one point against the horse.

So this certain horse was giving her problems trying to convert to a hunter horse and Jackie couldn't understand why. Jackie and her husband had asked some of the better riders to try the horse. After jumping two or three jumps, the horse would get very rambunctious and hard for all of them to control. He would even try to run away sometimes.

As a last resort, the trainer finally decided that he would get me to have a talk with the horse. The horse shared with me all of the places that he was sore, which were normal.

Then the trainer wanted me to ask the horse why he acts so weird in the ring? The horse's response to me very loudly was, *No one was watching the clock!*

I explained to the horse that there was no clock in the hunter ring like in the Grand Prix ring and that he could go as slow as his rider wanted him to. That afternoon Jackie had a class for the horse and she rode him. I noticed that all of the riders who couldn't handle the horse were peeking around the corner just to see how he went. He did perfect and she won!

THE WEE DOG WHO UNTIED THE GOVERNOR'S SHOELACES

We had been to the farm to speak with the horse this family owned and they were pleased with the results. A few weeks later we were invited to their home to speak with their three dogs. This family enjoyed living in a rather large home in a nice section of town. They were in the Virginia society circle and did a lot of entertaining which they enjoyed except for one thing that was always a bit of an annoyance. Ever since she was a puppy, one of their dogs who was four years old had enjoyed untying people's shoe laces. As I understood the problem, several prominent people had experienced having their shoelaces untied by Sally including the governor the night before our visit! It was by now a bit of a nuisance. We had a quick chat with all three dogs. We then spoke with one dog at a time. Sally's daughter was the first. She was beginning to learn to untie shoes but did not think it was as much fun as Sally told her it was. We asked what she liked and disliked about her living arrangement. She thought her mother, Sally was too strict with her and her brother would eat her food if she left any in her dish to go walk about. She also thought she should be allowed to go for more and longer walks.

Next we spoke with her brother Spencer. He was a real character. He reminded me of a college freshman with a nice car and enough money to take his girlfriend out on the town every weekend. He did not seem to have any worries and nothing to complain about. You could almost see him walking around in his sweater with the school colors and large letter. It seemed that when he wanted to go somewhere, he just went. There was an invisible fence in the yard but when he wanted to go somewhere he would just gather a lot of speed and run through it. Spencer the dog was much like a horse Fred Fletcher trained in New Zealand, a great trotting mare, owned by Sir Roy McKenzie named Deidre's Pride. When she wanted to graze on the other side of the electric fence, she would put her head down very low and run under the fence. She could undo most latches and manipulate chains almost as well as a human. She actually required a lock on the paddock gate in order to keep her in. Like Deidre's Pride, it seemed Spencer was good at opening latches and it was difficult to keep him in a confined area when you left home. Spencer did not get in much trouble when he got out but you never knew what he may be up to.

Now it was Sally's turn and she was ready. She talked about her children being spoiled by the lady of the house. The guests always played with them so she thought they played an important role in entertaining. I told her they did. I then explained that a lot of people did not like having their shoelaces untied by her. I explained that when she was a puppy this was considered entertaining but now that she was grown it was no longer fun. Sally listened very carefully then went over and sat in a corner by the sofa. She realized that what she thought was fun was causing a problem for her people. This was the end of that phrase of her life and I don't think Sally ever untied another shoelace. She *did* keep correcting her

children so that they would not be spoiled by guests.

175

THE REPEAT CLIENT WHO CALLED TOO LATE

One day I received a call from a man in South Boston, Virginia. He said I had helped him years ago with his mule, Ginny. Now he needed my help again. His horse was sick and had not eaten for a week. I told him that our fees had changed over the years and it was now $100. He said that was a lot of money and he would have to talk it over with his wife. I explained how draining it was to do this. I asked if anyone or anything had died recently as I was picking up a lot of sadness from the horse. The man told me an old hunting dog had died last week but he did not believe the horse knew him.

He asked me if the horse wanted to be put down because he turned and gave him a very sad look when he had left the horse that afternoon. The horse said he did not want to be put down. I conveyed this to him and then did a quick check of the horse's kidneys and liver. Both were in poor condition. I suggested some apple cider vinegar for the kidneys and some yogurt for the liver. We discussed how to give the vinegar and I told him he could sprinkle it over some oats and the horse might then eat the oats. I suggested he stand in front of the horse eating the yogurt and then put some on a spoon for the horse. If the horse ate it, he could put the balance in the feed tub. I told him to call a vet and he said, "My wife is a vet."

I was very disappointed that his wife was a vet and he did not want to spend a hundred dollars to find out what was wrong with his horse. I know from experience that we are much better than most vets at diagnosing lameness problems in horses, but not necessarily better at diagnosing sickness. I thought she should have been able to diagnose this. He said his wife only worked for another vet and she was not making very much money. He said the horse seemed to have something in its throat because he could smell a bad odor there. I had a quick look and saw it was on the right side just below the jaw. He asked if it was cancer and I dowsed a *no.*

I told him he was going to have to pay me if I was going be using my energy to work with his horse. He said he would call me back after talking with his wife. I told him we were good but not able to bring animals back from death. We talked about various things for about 30 minutes.

Suddenly someone came in the house crying. His horse had just died. He said, "I just waited to long to call you."

I told him I was sorry and we hung up. As it turned out, we most likely would not have saved the horse if we had done a complete reading, as it was too far gone.

Testimonial
CHARLIE & THE FIRE

Call Bill!

After Charlie had been here a couple of months we had a storm that knocked down several trees as well as many limbs. We cut the large branches and trunks for firewood and piled up the little stuff to burn. Charlie could look out of his stall window and watch us. The fire burned well into the night with no problems. However, in the morning when there was no fire left, just coals, Charlie was "crazy" in the stall. He tried to push the walls down and walked or ran in circles. First words from everyone - "Call Bill!"

Bill found out that Charlie's buddy died in a fire and the smell of the coals reminded him of seeing his friends' body after the fire. We knew we needed to move Charlie to the other side of the barn so Bill asked who would change stalls with him. Only Carlton was willing and only for two days. We had to beg him for a third day, but Charlie now has his stall on the other side of the barn.

Maria and Faye

FROM LOTTSBURG TO HAWAII

That Saturday began innocently enough. I was going to Ace Hardware in Lottsburg to pick up a trash cart I had ordered. Before leaving home I rang Calvin Keyser at Keyser Brothers Seafood to see if he had any crabmeat. Almost as soon as I left home I realized I had forgotten how to get to the new hardware store *and* Keysers. When I had my janitor and paper supply business Wardico, Keyser's was a good customer but I had not been on any of these back roads for years and they had changed a bit with a lot more people living on the water now. I knew the hardware store would have a sign so I drove to Lottsburg. I first turned down the road they used to be on but realized a different business was in their old building. I drove further down the main road and there they were. Waiting for my cart, I asked for directions to Keysers.

I found Calvin in the picking room. He soon recalled who I was. We had a talk about the difficulties of operating a small business today. He said he thought he was giving up on crab picking and try raising oysters in cages on his oyster grounds.

Hawaii Client Calling

When I got back to my truck and checked my phone, there was a message from a client in Honolulu, Hawaii. One of their dogs had gone missing. These folks have a night club near the Waikiki. The dog Lucy always goes in with Elaine around four a.m. to close up. This night everyone was busy cleaning and did not notice that the back door was left open and Lucy had gone out that way. Lucy is a Rhodesian Ridge Back dog. There are not a lot of those around but I get to listen to her almost every year when in Hawaii. These folks are good clients as they have two dogs, a cat and a horse. Almost as soon as they told me the story of her missing I could see her going out the door and off to the left. They later verified this as someone had seen her on the street headed in that direction. I told them I would go home and print out a map of the area. I requested a photo of Lucy and an exact address that she left from.

When I booted up my computer at home, the information was not there but arrived shortly after a phone call. I pointed out the information and Ann and I both had a look for Lucy. We were in different rooms but located her in the same area, near Kuhio Park. Elaine immediately left for the area which was a mile away. There was a ridgeback like Lucy in the back of a truck but it was not Lucy. There is a police station on the beach in Waikiki and since I told them I could see a man with her, the police began asking homeless people around if they had seen Lucy. No Luck. About two hours later they rang back to say Lucy was home. A bartender at another club was walking home about the time Lucy escaped. He picked her up and took her home with him. She had a collar but no ID on the collar. He made a couple of phone calls and was told the dog probably belonged at the club owned by my clients. By now the club was closed so he found out where they lived and was taking Lucy home. Walking her on the sidewalk near the house where she lived he was accosted by a neighbor who thought he was trying to steal her.

He wound up giving Lucy to the neighbor.

GEORGE
STEINBRENNER

Owner of the New York Yankees, he bought one of the foals of Carlisle Blaze for around 50,000 and we were staying in Fort Lauderdale, Florida, at the same hotel as the Yankees. One day when I saw Mr. Steinbrenner, I asked him how the filly was doing and he told me that she was doing okay. He had just bought the New York Yankees and we asked him how that experience was for him and he replied, "I have inherited the biggest bunch of damn babies that I've ever seen!"

It was irritating to him if they wouldn't play if they had an ache or pain, hurt finger, etc. They won't even take a chance to catch a ball and fall down. "I'm going to trade all of them!" The horse trainer was backing him up.

The trainer for the new horse called me in March and told me how good the filly was doing. He said, "I just trained her in last quarter in 29" [seconds] and that was way too fast.

You cannot train a young horse too fast. It ruins the cartilage in their knees. Their knees have a spot in them where there is a gap that doesn't come together when they are young. Most trainers don't like to start with a horse until the horse is at least four. But because of economics they have to start early.

THE GREAT BILLY HOUGHTON & DELVIN MILLER

Delvin Miller was known as harness racing's good will ambassador for many years. I was fortunate to meet him early, when l worked on the Maryland harness racing circuit as paddock and patrol judge. Many of the best two- and three-year-old standardbreds in the country come through Maryland for Grand Circuit Week at Rosecroft Raceway. Delvin and the famous harness driver, Billy Houghton, took a liking to me and were willing to answer most of my many questions regarding driving and training a horse.

Later in my life when I gave up working at the racetrack yet still owned horses, Delvin and Billy would always answer questions. I would usually have one or two horses with a few problems that my trainer did not seem to be able to find or correct. If necessary, Delvin and Billy would sometimes train these horses a mile to try to determine the problem. Then they would suggest ways to solve it. Most of the time I had purchased horses with poor conformation and they could not stand up to the rigors of training.

When I learned to dowse, I did not own any horses, but was still interested in them. In 1994 I attended dowsing school in Lyndonville, Vermont, where two horses were brought in for a class. There were the same 20 questions for each horse and I did not do to well. I believe I got seven answers right for one horse and eight for the other. Later after a great deal of practice, l learned to do a lot better. One of the things I learned was that you did not need to be with the physical horse in order to communicate with it.

One day I rang Delvin to tell him of my newly found dowsing abilities. He was nice but skeptical. He invited me up to The Meadows Raceway for Adios Day. Adios was one of the best stallions in the history of the sport and had helped make Delvin a wealthy man. The annual Adios Memorial Race was always raced on Adios Day. Sir Roy McKenzie from New Zealand was in the country so Delvin invited him also.

Invitation to New Zealand

Sir Roy was the person who first persuaded us to visit New Zealand. At the time, we were planning an eight week trip to Australia and Sir Roy told Delvin not to let us come that close to New Zealand without spending at least two weeks there. I flew up to Pittsburgh, rented a car and found the track without any major problems. The roads up there around Pittsburgh were so full of potholes that, compared to our part of Virginia, you would have thought you were in another country. We had a nice lunch at the track and later a more relaxed dinner at a quiet restaurant. I was excited that I could finally find out something about a horse without asking someone else. Delvin also thought that it was about time I learned something about horses. Now maybe I would not be calling him every time one of my horses had a problem!

Going Over Horses For Delvin

Delvin gave me a couple of his horses to go over while we were in the restaurant. We were able to pick up on most everything Delvin was aware of as a problem with both horses. I told him we could apply this ability to yearlings and avoid most of the type of yearlings I had been buying. We could pick up on conformation problems and weak areas without ever seeing the horse.

A few weeks later, Delvin sent me a sales catalog for a Kentucky yearling sale and asked us to go over a few yearlings for him. We went over the yearlings and sent him the information. He then went to the sale and saw that we were right on with most of the yearlings. We had been able, from a distance, to point out conformation faults you could see, as well as problems that you may not see unless looking specifically for them. We could even tell a horse's heart score and attitude from a distance.

For the next couple of years, I stayed in touch with Delvin by phone but mostly by letters typed by his secretary of many years, Gloria. Always signed and dictated from Florida but not read. Almost every year he offered me a breeding deal of a trotting stallion that he was not able to use. He would always say, "Just give me part of the profits from the yearling when you sell it." Unfortunately for us there were never any profits from these breedings. I think we got one live foal with these arrangements and that one only brought about $3000 in the yearling sale.

Delvin Decides He's Done With the Horses

One day I received a call from Delvin and he told me he had decided to get out of the horse racing business. He said he was getting too old for all of the traveling and the headaches involved with a racing stable. He said he might train one or two that he and a groom could care for but that was all he was going to do. At the time Jimmy Arthur was his trainer of note. Jimmy had assisted Delvin for years, until he decided to go out on his own. Now they were united again.

Delvin said he had six or seven head training at Garden State Raceway in New Jersey that he wanted to sell. He had some buyers coming over from Europe and each horse seemed to have some minor problems. He asked if I would be available to come to Garden State and have a look at these horses to see if we could sort out their problems. I was so excited that he had asked me for help that I could not have said anything but "When would you like me to come?"

Freehold Raceway in New Jersey

He asked if I could come up the next week as some of the horses were racing at Freehold that weekend. I told him that considering all he had done for me over the years, the only thing I would ask is that he pay my expenses. He said if we helped his horses and he sold them he would send me a little extra.

I arrived there just about noon and at the security gate I asked for the Delvin Miller stable. The guard made an announcement and soon Delvin drove up. He asked if I had eaten lunch and since l had not we went to a nearby restaurant for lunch. We had not seen each other for a year or so and there was a lot to chat about. After lunch we returned to the track and went to the barn to meet Jimmy Arthur.

Delvin introduced us and then left to take care of some

other business. Mr. Arthur did not remember me but I remembered him as he was Delvin's right-hand-man when they used to come through Maryland. He was very skeptical of what I could do. I explained that I still did not know much about horses but had some great Angels who did.

We went over to the first horse and we began to listen. We told Mr. Arthur a few things about this horse that he already knew and some things he was not aware of. As with most trainers, he was pleased we found things he already knew about but did not really want to hear about the things we found that he did not know about.

By the time we got to the last horse, Mr. Arthur was mellowing and beginning to ask some questions, especially about the things he heard that he did not know. l could tell he was going to use some of this information to help these horses. He was now somewhat amazed that we could pick up these sore places just from looking at the horse.

After finishing with the last horse we sat in some lawn chairs under a tree. We talked about great horses and people from years ago that these folks who were all older than I, could remember. It was a most enjoyable afternoon. Around 4:30 the group split up to go and feed their horses. Delvin arrived and Jimmy went over each horse with him. Delvin decided what to do for each, and as usual, the vet was called. Racehorse people in these days seldom took the time to rub their horses and ask their Angels to make them well. They just called the vet and asked for injections and shots.

Delvin told me that one of the trainers had told him about this motel close by and we would go there for a room. I was to follow him to the place. We pulled in to the motel and there were three cars in the parking lot sitting up on cinder blocks. In the office and there were bars in the clerk's window. Delvin asked the room rates and then paid for two rooms.

Fleeing the Bad Motel

We were given adjoining rooms. Right in front of my room was another car with the wheels off sitting on the ground. The dresser only had two drawers and one of them had part of the front broken out. The carpet was filthy and there was a black spot about three feet round in the middle of the floor. In the bathroom there were two dirty towels in the tub and one clean one on the rack. I walked outside and knocked on Delvin's door. His room was a little better but he didn't even have a clean towel in his room. He didn't see that as a problem as he could get some towels from the office.

There was a Holiday Inn within walking distance so we decided to walk there for dinner. When we finished dinner I went to the front desk and inquired about a room. Almost twice what we were paying at the other place. I told Delvin he could stay at the other place but I was going to shift to the Holiday Inn. Delvin decided that if we could share a room at the Holiday Inn, he would do it, and he was able to talk the desk clerk into issuing a credit to his credit card.

We were going to share a room with two double beds. I was a bit nervous staying in the same room with one of my idols. We were going to bed early so we could get up early. Just before going to sleep Delvin informed me that he expected me to stay all day Friday. Then on Saturday I could drive him to Freehold and stay with him for the weekend of racing.

Facing A Real Quandary

This request presented me with a real problem. I did not like being on the road for a holiday weekend. When planning the trip, we knew the six or seven horses he had would only take three or four hours. We had arranged with some friends in Potomac, Maryland, to be there on Friday afternoon to shift a stream from under their house and try to change a negative energy field. The stream was running under their dog's bedroom and causing him to be very uncomfortable there.

I told Delvin that to the best of my recollection we had not mentioned staying over the weekend before so I felt obligated to keep my appointment in Maryland. He did not seem to understand my problem and asked me to think about it and let him know in the morning. This really put me in a most difficult position. I would love to spend a weekend with

Delvin Miller. It was an honor for me to be asked. I had only brought one change of clothes so if I stayed I would need to purchase some clothes.

All night I tossed and turned, trying to decide. When we were eating breakfast the next morning it came to me that there would likely be another opportunity to spend some time with Delvin, so when he asked what I had decided, I told him he would need to find another driver.

A Rough Day at the Track

When I am doing this work of communicating with animals I need to get a good night's rest. Since I had very little rest the previous night, l was not able to hear anything that morning. We went to the track so Delvin could see the horses train. One of the horses came out on the training track so lame that it could hardly get around the track. It was very embarrassing for me but I was not able to hear anything and had absolutely no idea where the horse was sore.

Unfortunately for us, this was the ammunition Jimmy Arthur

needed to claim I was a fake.

Towards the end of the next week I received a letter from Delvin, thanking us for our help and telling me he had sold his horses. One of them sold for around $100,000 and others for nice sums. Included in the envelope was, as promised, a nice check.

We corresponded and spoke on the phone a couple of times but l did not get to see him again. Had I known I would not see him again, l would undoubtedly have stayed over the weekend with him while we were in New Jersey.

BILL GOES ON VACATION

It had been 20 years since I had taken a vacation. I remember studying about Australia when I was in the 7th grade and had always wanted to go there. So that is where I decided to take my first trip in a very long time. At that time, I owned harness horses and had become friends with a harness horse trainer named Delvin Milller who was known as the Good Will Ambassador of Harness Racing in the United States. Delvin trained horses for among others, Sir Roy McKenzie. I first met Mr. McKenzie at the Meadowlands Raceway in Washington, Pennsylvania, when he came to check on his horses. Delvin invited me to come up and have dinner with him and Mr. McKenzie. I believe that it was the same night as the 100,000 Adios Pace. Adios was a famous pacer that Delvin had owned and trained. I seemed to hit it off with Mr. McKenzie. We had our itinerary all planned and set out to spend a few weeks in Australia.

When Sir Roy McKenzie found out we were coming to

Australia he said, "Bill, you can't spend all of your vacation in Australia. You've got to come to New Zealand for at least two weeks if you are going to Australia!"

When Ann and I arrived in Australia, Sir Roy contacted me and said that he had changed my entire itinerary for New Zealand. Sir Roy said that he saw no need for us to come to the North Island. He would fly down to meet us in Christchurch. We found that the water in Australia was not that good. I remember that on our first day in New Zealand, we drank at least three pitchers of water!

The first day in New Zealand we drove to Roydon Lodge, which was Sir Roy's farm named after Roy and brother Don. Don lost his life in the Second World War. I believe being shot down in his bomber. Murray Steel was the farm manager. His wife, Ruth, also helped when the farm was busy. They had two young girls, Elizabeth and Victoria. We returned to the Roydon Lodge. The girls would go out in the morning and have tea with their "friends," or Angels. They would come in and tell us how their friends were dressed, what they talked about, and what they did. As far as playing, unfortunately, when Elizabeth started school, the teacher told her that she would have to leave her friends at home.

Testimonial

I recently contacted Mr. Northern via email about two of my horses and he agreed to help me. I had never heard of animal communication before. However, after hearing him on [a radio show], I decided to give him a try. Due to the sensitive nature of part of the information he obtained for me, he called me Friday from Virginia, rather than email; however, he did email a report after our conversation, minus the sensitive info. We talked for about a half an hour! Mr. Northern gave me numerous, specific, 100% accurate information and told me things he could not possibly know. He even described my horses' personalities completely accurately! One remarkable thing he told me was that one of my horses had back pain, and Bill described in detail where his back was bothering him. The day before the phone call from Mr. Northern, we had the vet out for something else. The vet discovered a sore spot on my horse's back just where Bill said it was the next day! Mr. Northern also gave me his home phone number and asked me to call him if I need any further information at no charge! He was absolutely wonderful to talk to. He was kind, compassionate, and spoke with great concern regarding my horses. At the end of the phone call I asked him if he would like me to send him some money for the phone call. His response was, No. He said he doesn't usually telephone people with reports, but due to the sensitive nature of part of this report, he felt the need to call me. Talking to him was a life-changing experience for me! I believe Mr. Bill Northern is The Real Deal.

Kristen Marelich, Redding, CA

204

Bill Northern's Dowsing School

GETTING STARTED

Welcome to what we hope you will consider to be one of the best days of your life. You will be doing things today that as of now, you quite likely consider impossible for you to do. Physicists are able to explain it through Quantum Mechanics. But few are actually able to do it. Moses was probably the most well-known of dowsers because he led the Jewish people through the desert for 40 years, all the time locating food and water for them. The Aboriginal people of Australia are still doing this.

There are four basic tools used in dowsing. We have "Y" rods, "L" rods, the pendulum, and the bobber. These tools come in many forms.

We will begin our day by going outside and locating underground veins of water, electric, telephone and water pipes. Each of these has a slightly different feeling and you should attempt to let your body feel the difference between each. You do not have to actually feel the difference today but be aware of it.

Next will be the most important thing you will learn: Putting a field of God's protective light around you and others to protect them from harmful thought forms and other undesirable things. This you will use everyday.

After lunch, you will learn to program your pendulum. It is very important that you learn to do this as this is how your Angels and spirit guides will be communicating with you.

Map dowsing is done the same way whether you are looking for negative or noxious energy, lost animals, water, etc.

The same is true for going over animals to locate problem areas. We will ask you to draw your house or property then dowse it for any detrimental energy. We will discuss the importance of thought forms and if we are up to it, we will go outside and dowse some thought forms that we as a group place for a class member to locate.

You will need to practice 15 - 20 minutes a day until you are comfortable with dowsing. You can play something like solitaire and dowse the best card to move.

Dowse cards: have two of the same color and one of another. Then turn them over and look for the odd card using a dowsing tool. You can also use your fingers for dowsing these. Rubbing your thumb against your fingers. For me, slippery is *yes* and sticky is *no.*

ANIMAL COMMUNICATION: HOW WE WORK

Everything in the universe has a special frequency. We endeavor to tune in to the frequency of each animal we want to work with whether in person or remotely. Sometimes we hear the animal's voice and sometimes they just seem to guide our eyes to where they believe they need our attention. Sometimes they may not know the name of what it is that troubles them so they do their best to show us.

We are not vets and know very little about medicine. However, one of my Angels is Dr. Angus McDonald who was an excellent vet. He often guides us to the solution. He still seems able to help us diagnose lameness issues quite well. We do our best to listen carefully to the animal and are usually able to pinpoint what is causing the problem. Often we are able to suggest proper treatment. We try not to use pharmaceutical solutions if something else appears to work as well. Quite often a bit of rubbing and asking the Angels to fix it is all that is necessary to solve the problem. We are often able to negotiate behavior issues, provided the two-legged is willing to work with and try to understand the four-legged and prepared to give a little also.

Our basic fee is 300 per hour. About the same as most professionals. We work in increments of ten minutes. A ten minute reading is 60. A 20 minute reading is 100. Extra minutes are 5. The tuning in and listening is very draining. Therefore, we have a limit of one animal a day for remote readings. And we have a limit of about 90 minutes a day for in person animals. We will appreciate your having your payment ready when we are finished with your friend. This helps us get to the next animal more quickly. They do not like to wait anymore than we do.

Thank you for allowing us to help you and your friend.

MAP DOWSING

Through what is known as map dowsing, you are able to mark well sites for people and find energy fields on property anywhere in the world while sitting at your desk at your home. This can also be used to locate missing people provided they want to be found. We often use this method to search for lost and missing animals. We always first like to have a photo of the animal or person we are looking for. From this photo, we can usually determine if the subject is still alive in this realm. If we are not able to detect any energy, we tell the client that we have not picked up anything to lead us to the subject. I try not to tell people that the person or animal is dead because I have found that if the subject does not wish to be located, or perhaps for another reason we may not be able to pick up on their energy if they want to hide.

If we find the subject to be alive, we then take a map out of the area in which the animal left from. It's very important to know the starting point. Go over it in one of the many ways to map dowse. I usually use a straight edge and run it across the paper from left to right. As soon as my pendulum swings to a yes, I will stop and draw a line along the straight edge, next I will put the straight edge at the bottom of the page and go up slowly until the pendulum swings. I then draw another line and where these lines cross is usually where the missing object is at that time.

Where the lines cross, you can check each corner to see if the subject is moving in that direction by putting your finger or pointer there and asking if the subject is moving that way.

We have found it very important to have the exact address of the place the subject went missing from. If you have this information and are able to mark this exact spot on the map, you can move on.

Now, when we locate the subject we can draw a line from the home to the subject. Put arrows on the line to show the subject the correct way to go. It is very important to have it marked correctly because the subject will often go right past it if not marked properly. You can also draw an oval outside the line in case the subject gets off course. Draw arrows in this case. That way they will know which way to go when they get to it.

We have made the mistake of not marking home correctly and the animals have come first to where we marked and not finding anything familiar, they kept on going.

Another thing to remember is that dogs are almost constantly moving. If they are lost they will be looking for the way home. Sometimes, they left where they were because they were not happy and don't want to put up with this anymore.

When a dog is lost, it will be on the lookout for anything familiar that may relate to home. This can be a property marker, another animal, a person or a car. Even the energy lines you draw will help them tune into where they need to go.

If the dog left because it was unhappy and does not wish to return it will be looking for a new home. Sometimes, the dog is lucky enough to hook up with a house that needs a dog. Sometimes the dog will be able to connect with another dog or a pack of dogs.

When in a pack, dogs are stronger and able to catch and kill animals that would likely get away from just one dog. Packs of dogs can be very dangerous, so always be careful if you encounter a pack of dogs.

Some dogs are afraid of people and don't want to be put in the same situation again. These dogs will be seen around dumps and anywhere a bit of food can be found. These are the dogs the animal warden us usually called to catch and take away.

Not all pound dogs are good candidates for adoption. You can and should always ask an animal communicator if this will be the right animal for you. If not, don't be saddened, just keep looking for another that will be better suited to you.

Most dogs will try to adapt to the way that you and your family live. We rarely think that it is a good idea for families with children under 3 years old to adopt a dog. Some children may need to be as old as 6 before they learn to properly relate to an animal. Most dogs will put up with a lot of abuse from children but will eventually bite if continually provoked. Not all people enjoy small children and neither do all animals. Some have a lot more patience than others.

As a rule, cats will not put up with much abuse from anyone. Adults, as well as children, need to treat cats with the same respect or they will simply run away at the first opportunity. Most cats are very capable of providing for themselves and really do not need to put up with abuse from anyone.

Most of the time, people call us to look for missing cats and we find they left for a reason and are not really lost.

When we inform these people that their cats left because they are mad, the first response is almost always, "Oh, that couldn't be so." Then after a few minutes and some thought, they will say something like, "I'll bet it is because of the new puppy or the new cat or perhaps the grandchildren."

Cats will often forgive you if you are willing to promise them that you will correct the situation that caused them to

216

leave. Dowsing is a wonderful experience for those that are willing to learn how to do it and can actually change your whole outlook on life.

HOW TO FIND LOST ANIMALS

When I teach dowsing, I always teach people how to find lost animals. With this method, you can find just about anything. I don't remember who exactly taught me, but I learned at one of the dowsing conferences. I got really good at it, to the point to where I was getting calls from all over the world from people asking me to find their lost pets. One time, when I went to New Zealand, I received a call from some people asking if they could come to see me and bring lunch. Then they proceeded to tell me the story of how I had found their lost dog when they called me in the U.S.

You need to know the animal's name, the exact address of where the animal left, and what kind of animal it is. Then, ideally you would print out a map of the area, mark on the map where the animal left from. Next, take out your pendulum (or whatever your dowsing tool of choice is) and start at the spot where the pet was last seen. You move your finger either direction and ask your pendulum if the pet went this way. If it gives you a yes, then you continue with your finger in that direction. If it gives you a no, you go in another direction until you get a yes.

Keep in mind, whenever you are looking for an animal, the first thing that you do is ask your guides if the animal is still alive. If the guides say *Yes*, you continue. If the guides say *No*, I tell the client that I am not able to connect with the animal at this time.

A couple of months before, they had contacted me asking if I could locate their lost dog. And so I did. I gave them the location of where I thought that the dog was (near a train tracks) and they found him there, deceased. He was within one meter of exactly where I had pinpointed his location. In this particular case, I was able to locate the dog because he had just been killed and his energy was still there for me to pick up on.

FINDING A LOST ANIMAL WITHOUT A MAP

One morning, early, we were on our way to the airport to go to New Zealand when I got a call from a regular client, his name was Harold Williams and he was from Petersburg. This man owned six Irish Setters and they had a tendency to go walk-about or run away. He told me three of the dogs were missing. So on the way to the airport, I took out my pendulum. In this instance, I didn't have a map, but I had worked for him many times before, so I knew the property. I pinpointed exactly where he was, what direction to drive in, and before I arrived at the airport, he located his three dogs.

The unique thing about Harold was that, unlike some clients, he understood how difficult it was to locate his dogs. He always not only paid me for finding the dogs, he paid me double, to cover the next time that they got lost!

THE TOPP SISTERS

On the south island of New Zealand, I met lady named Linda Topp. She was a well-known country singer in New Zealand with a group called The Topp Singers. She invited me to dinner. Her home was located towards Stavley, a mountainous area.

Linda liked to hunt and fish. She took hunting and fishing parties out and was very good at it. One day, she called and said that her dogs had gone missing. I printed out a map of the area, started looking for them, and found them, not where they usually would go, but down the road around seven kilometers. I told her that they were lying under a tree at that time, sleeping. She couldn't believe it, but she got into her car and drove 7 kilometers to where I told her to, when she arrived at the spot that I had told her, there were the dogs, lying there under the tree asleep. She was elated.

TIP FROM BILL: **Here is the key.** She followed my instructions immediately, she didn't hesitate. Dogs travel. If she had waited, they probably would not have been in the same location as I had found them. Here is an example of what I'm talking about.

DOGS TRAVEL

This story is regarding a lost dog in Tappahannock, Virginia. I had the client send a picture of the dog to me and tell me where it had left from. I located the dog and it appeared as though it was near a school on Airport Road. I told her where it was. So she waited for her lunch break, and then went to look for the dog. The people at the school confirmed that they had seen her dog, but it was no longer there.

So she called me again. I dowsed again, and this time the dog was located across town at the hospital. I told her where it was located and again, she waited. She decided to go to look for her dog when she got off from work. The people at the hospital told her that they had seen the dog there, but it was now gone.

She called again, and once again, I was able to find the area where the dog was located. The people that lived near the spot where I located it had taken the dog into their home. I wasn't aware that the dog was in a home, I just knew the location. She checked with neighbors, and sure enough, the dog was in a nearby home, as I had specified.

It was very frustrating to find the dog and have her call me to say that she couldn't locate it. She waited both times that I located her dog. When she called me to tell me that she had finally found her dog, I told her, "That's great, I'm glad that you found the dog, but please don't ever call me again!"

A SAD STORY OF
THE LOST MONKEY

I received a call from a client whose pet monkey had gone missing from a trailer in the desert of New Mexico. It seems that the owner had cancer and had to be hospitalized for a few weeks. Naturally, she couldn't leave the monkey alone, so she asked a cousin, who lived out in the desert, to look after him for her. It was customary to let the monkey out of the cage most of the time, during the day, as long as the doors and windows were closed. It seems that the cousin forgot that the monkey was loose and opened the door, and the monkey was gone. The cousin spent a few hours looking for the monkey, but couldn't find it. He then called the owner and told her what had happened.

She called me and asked me if would look for the monkey. So I asked her to give me that address where the monkey left from. Then I printed out a map and began to dowse. I found where I thought that the monkey was, but the caretakers did not believe that he went the way that I had told her. When she called me the next day to tell me that they had still not found the monkey, I dowsed again and told her that the monkey was still in the same area, but that at night he could see lights. Again, the caretakers thought that the monkey was in a different direction, so they didn't look where I had said that he was. Then, on the third day, they finally looked where I had told them to and they found the monkey's skeleton. He had been picked by the buzzards. He was right where my Angels and I had said that he was.

TEACHING THE VETERINARIAN, DR. BARBER

We were at the horse show in Upperville, Virginia, and I was working with a few horses. I found that one horse had a stifle problem. The owner had had the vet come to inject the horse's stifles, but I was still picking up that there was a problem. There was a man that wanted to see how we did things, and I had no idea that it was Dr. Barber, the Official Veterinarian of the Hits Horse Shows. He asked me to please put my finger on the spot that hurt, which I did. Afterwards, I went to work on other horses. Later on, I found out that the man that I was showing my dowsing to was Dr. Barber. He told people that stifles had three points in which you can inject. He had already injected two of them. I had put my finger on the spot where the third injection needed to go. I had no idea that the horse had already been injected. For this reason, Dr. Barber started taking lessons from me.

ANIMALS ARE NOT AFRAID TO DIE

Several times a year, clients will ring me to ascertain whether their four-legged friend is now ready to cross over. Animals instinctively know that there is something better waiting for them when they cross over. They are sent to us to teach us something we need to learn. We may not know what it is that we are supposed to learn, but they do. In New Zealand, I often follow a truckload of sheep being taken to the freezer works. They have known, somehow all of their lives, that they would be making this trip, but they are not afraid. Some actually look forward to leaving.

Pets are the same. Sometimes they have not finished with us when they need to leave. We being afraid to die, try to keep them around as long as we can. When need to tell them how we will get along without them, what we will be doing and how. If you plan to get another pet, we need to take them to the pound to help select their replacement. You will be surprised at the attention they give to this job, particularly if you have told them that they are going to have the opportunity to select the next person to look after you.

TEACHING JOE SIX-PACK'S JOCKEY

James Graham was the first jockey that I ever taught. His wife took lessons at the same time that he did, as well as his trainer. James didn't practice like I had wanted him to. I taught James how to listen to horses. James was riding a horse called Joe Six-Pack. Joe had been a terrible horse to get along with. If you led him around the track, he wouldn't let anyone ride him. He didn't need one outrider, but two every morning while training. Thoroughbreds always train early morning, usually around 5 a.m. and stop around 10 a.m. After listening to Joe, he told me that the reason that he threw riders off and was unruly was because he was very sore. I told the chiropractor where Joe was hurting and after they worked on him, he started to get better. After a few weeks of therapy, he ended up being able to race again. Joe Six-Pack was one of these horses that liked to give it all that he had in the beginning of the race and then he would fizzle out towards the end. On this particular day, Joe was 45-1, which is a long shot.

James had told Joe that if he would let him rate him in the first part of the race that he would have him in a position at the top of the stretch to where he could win the race. Joe Six-Pack listened to James and missed winning the race by a hair. It was very close.

ASK THE RIGHT QUESTION

Ann and I were renting a flat in Christchurch. Near our flat, there was a 300 acre park in the middle of the city named Haggley Park. We would walk across the park to get downtown to Christchurch. One day, it looked like it was getting ready to rain and I asked my pendulum if it was going to rain. I got a *yes.* I thought that we needed to start walking back. Ann dowsed and asked the question, "Are we going to get wet?" She got a distinct *no.* We were half-way home and it began to rain, so we ran up under a big tree and guess what? We didn't get wet!

TIP FROM BILL: One Important Rule of Dowsing: Be careful how you ask the question!

HOW TO DOWSE
FOR A FRENCH COIL

Tony Gehringer, a dowsing instructor from New Mexico, taught me how to dowse a tree for a French Coil. A French Coil is a copper wire used to place an electromagnetic field around the tree to ward off insects and to promote healing that the tree needs.

First, you dowse and ask the tree how many wraps of wire it needs, it knows! Every tree has a front door and a back door. You can find the front door by dowsing. Just ask the tree and use your L-Rods and the rods will point to the edge of the door.

Using chalk, mark on the tree where the front door is and you wrap the copper wires around the tree depending on how many wraps it needs. The wire has to be "earthed" or grounded, for approximately 12 inches and then you begin to wrap it around the tree. When you get the proper about of coils, you leave part of the wire sticking up for an antennae, approximately six inches, and cut the wire. The next time that I went to New Zealand, I couldn't wait to share my new discovery.

First, I went to Polytech, in Christchurch and spoke to Holga Kohl who was in charge of the Organic Dept., and he agreed to let us put a coil around four trees and he would see how they looked the following year. When I went outside to the laboratory, I noticed that all of the people that were doing grafting, etc. had a copper wire in the pot with the plant, they were already using it to some extent. Since he was not extremely interested, I called Bob Crowder at Lincoln University in Lincoln, New Zealand. Bob was the most well known noted expert of Organic Farming in New Zealand. He told me to come on out and "we will give it a go!" I explained to him what it was and how we would do it and he organized enough copper wire for us to do approximately 20 trees. I was teaching Bob and the Woofers – the workers on the organic farm -- and they would take what they had learned and go back to where they came from to use their new knowledge.

This, of course, was new to everyone because at this time not many people had ever heard of this. We put the coil around various fruit trees that had poor fruit and weren't healthy. We let everyone have a go at doing the French Coil and some even tried to put the copper around the tree without dowsing it first to see how much difference it was the next year. When I returned to New Zealand the next year, one of the first places that I went to was Lincoln University. Bob was extremely impressed with the results of the French Coil. We decided that we would put a French Coil around more trees each year and the results were really good. We also tried putting a copper wire around the perimeter of a garden where the white moth was depositing eggs that were eating the vegetables. Each time that I visited, New Zealand I would assist with placing the French Coils until they closed down the Organic Department of the University. Speaking of New Zealand and Woofers, one day I was at Lincoln University and something was causing all of the walnut trees to have white spots on their leaves and the fruit. I told them that I thought that if we put a protective light around them that we could get rid of whatever was causing the problem. So I got one of the Woofers to go down to the walnut tree orchard with me and I told him that we were going to put an energy field around the trees, just as we had done with the fruit trees, to protect them.

First, he and I picked out one of the trees to put the light around. (No one else knew which one that we had picked.) Then I had him assist me in putting the light around the one tree that we had selected. He was a little skeptical, but assisted me, anyway. I asked, "Do you think that we have it right now?" He shook his head, *yes*

So I told him to go up and get the other Woofers and see if they could tell with their L-Rods which tree that we had put the light around. He and the others came down with their L-Rods and began to walk around the orchard. Almost every single one of them found the tree that we had put the light around. I went up to him and touched him on the shoulder and told him, "You did a good job."

He took off running scared to death and said, "Don't

touch me!"

When I was teaching a student in Christchurch how to dowse named Natalie Mallett, I noticed that she had a peach tree that had very tiny peaches on it. I had taught her how to put a light around herself, her house, and her car. I told her that she could put that same light around her peach tree. We also installed a French Coil around the tree and I asked her to please pay attention to how it worked for the next season. Along about December of the following year -- Summertime for New Zealand -- Natalie sent me a picture of her peach tree. the peaches on the tree were as big as softballs!

TALK TO YOUR ANIMAL FRIENDS

Animals don't like to suffer any more than we do. Having a leg removed to some is okay as long as they still get attention they desire. To others it may be a death sentence. You just have to pay attention as to how they are feeling.

Please let them pass over when they are ready. Try to have the vet give them what treatment they need, not to only stay alive but to have some quality life. Some vets will treat your friend as long as you authorize the treatment, even if it only means hanging on a few more days to live. They do this out of sympathy and to bring in more revenue. Today many people have medical insurance for animals. So if the insurance company will pay, the treatment is considered necessary. Three times I have been contacted by an insurance company to go over a horse and and ask her if she is ready to leave us. They all had life as well as medical insurance. All were insured for $500,000 to $1,500,000. I was never told the reason for these visits in advance. Two of the horses wanted to carry on, while the other was ready to leave.

Talk to your friend, they will understand. Tell them what your plans are for today and for the week, perhaps the month. We tell horses two or three weeks before a horse show so they can mentally prepare for it.

If you need to cut hair or trim nails, etc., start telling why you need to do that particular job a few days before you plan to do it.

Always do what you say you are going to do. Like a child, they will be looking forward to the time. If you fail too many times, they will not believe you.

Tell them your troubles and your triumphs. They listen and they really care. Remember, they are often your best friend.

Pay attention to how they are feeling and if you detect something wrong, start working on it now before it gets worse. Please don't put it off. They don't like going to the doctor anymore than you. So treat the problem early, if you know how.

BILL'S TALK TO A CHILDREN'S HARNESS RACING CLASS
February 23, 2015

I used to think animals were dumb.

I used to think they were supposed to do what I wanted them to do when I asked them to do it.

I now realize that they have the same thoughts and feelings we have but are unable to express them in our language.

Suppose you were taken from your mother when you were three years old. Then taken to another area where the language your mother spoke was not used at all.

My father died when I was only seven years old. I relate to this.

In general, animals are much like you. They want to please their people and will do so if their work is properly explained to them.

You need to speak to them as you would a three year

old child. Be careful to explain everything.

If they are not doing what you want them to do, it is likely because you have not done a very good job of explaining what it is you expect of them.

You should reward them with kind words, hugs, even treats when they do well and accept part of the blame when when they don't quite get the job done as you expect.

Do not lose your temper and hit them. They do not like to be hit anymore than you do. If they miss something explain the problem to them as you would like a problem explained to you.

Use dowsing to help determine where your horse may be sore, or where he does not feel well.

Practice dowsing over a stream, electric line or water line. Also practice with cards.

Also look into your animals' eyes and notice their facial expressions. When you learn to do this it will teach you a lot about people as well as animals.

Pay attention to the mistakes others make. Do not

gloat over their errors but learn from them and endeavor not to make the same mistakes.

When rubbing on a horse to help them, always have a strong intent that it will be fixed.

About the Author

Bill's globetrotting search for water and his healing of sick horses is a far cry from his early life in the United States where he grew up in Warsaw, a small town in Eastern Virginia. Growing up in Warsaw, Bill's lifelong love of horses developed. By modern standards he had a hard childhood. His father, who ran a general store in the town, died when Bill was just seven. Bill's mother, lacking sufficient business acumen to run the store, sold the business.

Life for Bill and his mother was a financial struggle. When he was 12, he began working 30 hours a week in his uncle's restaurant, fitting the work around school. Bill busied himself at the restaurant for five years, using the proceeds from some of his labors to get his uncle to buy him a typewriter he used as his ticket to better school marks. "My handwriting was not very good and you got better grades if you typed your assignments." he explains.

The effort paid off as Bill was awarded a scholarship to attend the University of Richmond. But he didn't use the time productively, he says. "I ended up spending most of my time playing poker, playing in a band, and shooting on the rifle team. I didn't work."

After another unsuccessful stint at a second university, Bill headed to Washington D.C. where he worked in a hotel and rubbed shoulders with some of the Capitol's movers and shakers before returning to Warsaw, where he set up his janitorial supplies business, Wardico.

He was drawn into the world of horse racing and working as a judge at racetracks. He has also owned between 30 and 35 trotters in his time, although he says he only ever owned one he would describe as successful.

That was before he discovered dowsing and developed his skills.

Bill ran Wardico for 25 years until he discovered dowsing. He subsequently retired from the business world to concentrate on dowsing. He traveled half the year to attend horse shows throughout the eastern United States during summer. In 1989, he started to travel to New Zealand to avoid harsh North American winters, although he says it's the warm, friendly people that are the biggest draw for him. He regularly stayed in Rakaia, a town he feels is similar in size to his hometown back in Virginia. He dabbled in real estate in New Zealand but gave up to devote his energies to filling dry wells and to horses.

Send correspondence to:
Bill Northern
P.O. Box 986
Warsaw, Virginia 22572
bill@billnorthern.com

Honey House Press + Book Hive works with aspiring authors to craft and sculpt chapbooks, novellas, and full-length books of any genre from informal writing.

Everyone has a story. We can help gather and tell your story or the life story of a loved one to reach any audience you want.

We will work with you every step of the way, or one step at a time. Email info@honeyhousehive.com or call 443-478-3080

www.honeyhousehive.com

Made in the USA
Columbia, SC
22 September 2021